LEADER SHIFT

A YEAR OF LEADERSHIP GOLD

by:

Dr. Gene Herndon

© 2020 Gene Herndon. All Rights Reserved. Unauthorized Duplication is Prohibited.

Copyright © 2020 Gene Herndon United States of America. All Rights Reserved under international copyright laws. Contents and/or cover may not be reproduced in whole or in part without prior written consent.

Printed in the United States of America

Published by Aion Multimedia
20118 N 67th Ave
Suite 300-446
Glendale AZ 85308
www.aionmultimedia.com

ISBN-13: 978-1-7330332-5-1

Scripture quotations marked (KJV) are taken from the King James Bible, New York: American Bible Society: 1999.

.Scripture quotations marked NLT are taken from the *Holy Bible*, New Living Translation, copyright © 1996, 2004, 2015 by Tyndale House Foundation. Used by permission of Tyndale House Publishers, Inc., Carol Stream, Illinois 60188. All rights reserved.

Scripture quotations marked MSG are taken from *THE MESSAGE*, copyright © 1993, 2002, 2018 by Eugene H. Peterson. Used by permission of NavPress. All rights reserved. Represented by Tyndale House Publishers, Inc.

Scripture quotations taken from the Amplified® Bible (AMPC), Copyright © 1954, 1958, 1962, 1964, 1965, 1987 by The Lockman Foundation Used by permission. www.Lockman.org

The Christian Standard Bible. Copyright © 2017 by Holman Bible Publishers. Used by permission. Christian Standard Bible®, and CSB® are federally registered trademarks of Holman Bible Publishers, all rights reserved. Scripture quotations taken from the New American Standard Bible® (NASB), Copyright © 1960, 1962, 1963, 1968, 1971, 1972, 1973, 1975, 1977, 1995 by The Lockman Foundation Used by permission. www.Lockman.org
"

TABLE OF CONTENTS

Who Is Dr. Gene?

Week 1 - 3 Things I Wish I Knew When I Started My Business	7
Week 2 - Gifts and Calling	11
Week 3 - Knowing Your Worth	17
Week 4 - Portable Vision for Clarity	21
Week 5 - Obstacle, or Opportunity?	27
Week 6 - Rinse and Repeat	31
Week 7 - Selling Sugar Water	35
Week 8 - The Tension of Being Unreasonable	39
Week 9 - The Time I Almost Quit	45
Week 10 - The Time I Almost Quit - Part 2	51
Week 11 - They Laughed @ Me	55
Week 12 - 6 Questions to Refocus	59
Week 13 - Champions Have Short Memory	65
Week 14 - Change Your Environment	69
Week 15 - Decision Fatigue	73
Week 16 - Eat More Peanuts	77
Week 17 - Open Door Policy	83
Week 18 - Productivity	89
Week 19 - Ship the Product	97
Week 20 - The Mystery of Mastery Revealed	101
Week 21 - Putting a Whiteboard in Your Wheelhouse	107
Week 22 - Why Pencils Have Erasers	111
Week 23 - The Spirit of Mammon	115
Week 24 - The First Three Letters in "Diet" are D-I-E	121
Week 25 - The $6-Million Mistake	125
Week 26 - Develop Your Team into Elite Players	129
Week 27 - Develop Your Team into Elite Players - Part 2	133
Week 28 - The Four C's of Recruiting	137
Week 29 - The Four C's of Recruiting - Part 2	143
Week 30 - The Four C's of Recruiting - Part 3	147
Week 31 - Getting Outside Help Training	153
Week 32 - If You Don't Have One, You Are One	159
Week 33 - Training People to Be Nice	163
Week 34 - Delegation: The Magic Bullet - Part 1	167
Week 35 - Delegation: The Magic Bullet - Part 2	171
Week 36 - Delegation: The Magic Bullet - Part 3	175
Week 37 - Delegation: The Magic Bullet - Part 4	181
Week 38 - Being the Guide	185
Week 39 - The Art of the Pivot	191

Week 40 - Not If You Mess Up, But When	195
Week 41 - 5 Keys to a Wealthy Mindset	199
Week 42 - 5 Keys to a Wealthy Mindset - Part 2	203
Week 43 - Feeling Stuck	207
Week 44 - Institutional Imperative	211
Week 45 - Kidpreneur	215
Week 46 - Leading in a Time of Crisis	221
Week 47 - Leading in a Time of Crisis - Part 2	225
Week 48 - Retail Apocalypse	229
Week 49 - May I Take Your Order, Please?	235
Week 50 - 12 Key Attributes of Elite Team Players	239
Week 51 - 12 Key Attributes of Elite Team Players - Part 2	245
Week 52 - Why We Do What We Do	251

Who Is Dr. Gene?

What's holding you back?
Do you sense there is more to your potential?
Do you feel like your life is sometimes misaligned or out of sync?
You are not alone.

It has been said that the two most important days of your life are the day you were born and the day you figure out why.

Many people go through life, not realizing or achieving the fullness of their God-given potential.

All my life, I've had a desire to help people and never truly understood why.

I felt destined to help people to do great things.

I believe if you have the right tools to work harder and smarter, you can create a compelling future—complete with satisfaction and fulfillment. Excuses are not acceptable.

I believe it is a sin against God to not walk in your full potential.

We at Gene Herndon Ministries are committed to making a difference locally and an impact globally.

Our mission is to equip, inspire, and influence extraordinary people, leaders, and organizations to impact the world for the glory of God.

We do that by
- Seeking the Lost
- Training the Found
- Sending the Ready
- Equipping the Sent

In today's fast-paced global economy, being good is not enough. You must be *great*. At your very core, you must desire to be prolific and produce much fruit; yours must be an organization of impact, creating efficacious results, and demonstrating excellence by being pre-eminent.

After 25 years of business experience and 15 years of ministry, I strive to live in accordance with these values every day. To me, success is all about my faith, those I love, and making a difference in the lives of those with whom God has seen fit to trust me.

We at Gene Herndon Ministries are here to help. Together we can dent the world for the cause of Christ. We believe that in the end, our lives mustn't be about money or things. True life is about being a difference-maker in the kingdom of God. Level up!

You are stronger than you know
smarter than you think and
greater than your past.

Who Is Dr. Gene?

What's holding you back?
Do you sense there is more to your potential?
Do you feel like your life is sometimes misaligned or out of sync?
You are not alone.

It has been said that the two most important days of your life are the day you were born and the day you figure out why.

Many people go through life, not realizing or achieving the fullness of their God-given potential.

All my life, I've had a desire to help people and never truly understood why.

I felt destined to help people to do great things.

I believe if you have the right tools to work harder and smarter, you can create a compelling future—complete with satisfaction and fulfillment. Excuses are not acceptable.

I believe it is a sin against God to not walk in your full potential.

We at Gene Herndon Ministries are committed to making a difference locally and an impact globally.

Our mission is to equip, inspire, and influence extraordinary people, leaders, and organizations to impact the world for the glory of God.

We do that by
- Seeking the Lost
- Training the Found
- Sending the Ready
- Equipping the Sent

In today's fast-paced global economy, being good is not enough. You must be *great*. At your very core, you must desire to be prolific and produce much fruit; yours must be an organization of impact, creating efficacious results, and demonstrating excellence by being pre-eminent.

After 25 years of business experience and 15 years of ministry, I strive to live in accordance with these values every day. To me, success is all about my faith, those I love, and making a difference in the lives of those with whom God has seen fit to trust me.

We at Gene Herndon Ministries are here to help. Together we can dent the world for the cause of Christ. We believe that in the end, our lives mustn't be about money or things. True life is about being a difference-maker in the kingdom of God. Level up!

You are stronger than you know
smarter than you think and
greater than your past.

WEEK 1

3 Things I Wish I Knew When I Started My Business

We polled our Leadership Uncensored family and asked this question: What one thing would I tell any new ministry leader or entrepreneur or someone who is climbing the corporate ladder?

Here is how our poll's respondents answered, plus my overachiever insights.

First of all, you need to value your education and development. I don't necessarily mean formal education and degrees from institutions of learning (though I am the president of a Christian university). But I am speaking of personal development. Years ago, my pastor at the time told me to never spend more on what you put "on" yourself than what you put "in" yourself. Your development is critical, and you must take it seriously and invest in it to reach higher and greater levels of accomplishment. I assure you, it is *what you don't know that will cost you.* You must develop *a personal development plan and budget.*

Here is a good template:

- Spend time figuring out the *top two skills* you need to develop and improve to be successful.
- Research and find *three books on that specific subject.*
- Then find *two books about the particular business, vertical, or ministry you have chosen* to focus on.
- Order all five of them at once so that you have them in your possession to refer to as needed.
- *Research conferences* you would benefit from and *register for one.*

Now you have *a personal development plan.* I have been the senior pastor of only one church, yet I have pastored many churches. Here's how: As I grew, our church evolved, developed, and changed as well.

Secondly, *learn the value of time.* Figure out how much money you would like to make per year and divide it by 2,000. This number roughly represents the working hours in a year. This calculation will give you an estimate of what your time is worth. When you decide what you are going to do with your time, use this figure as a guide.

If, for instance, you are doing some task for which you could pay someone else less than what it costs you in working hours lost, defer it, delete it, or delegate it. Everyone has the same amount of time (24 hours in a day), but the difference between the financially successful and the unsuccessful is that the astute have learned to allocate that time better and invest it into activities that produce higher results.

For example, let's say you spend an extra 10 to 15 minutes driving around town looking for cheaper gas. If your income goal is $200,000 per year, your time is worth $1.66 per minute. If gas costs, let's say, $3 per gallon, you would have to find some at almost half off to recover the amount spent trying to find it. Realistically, you might save a few cents, but you'll have spent nearly $25 doing so.

Here's another example. Getting my car detailed costs me $150. My skilled detailer does it in about four hours. It would take my unskilled self six hours to do the job. Again, using the 200K number as my income goal, it would cost me $600 to do what I can pay someone else $150 to do for me. That doesn't even take into consideration the opportunity costs of what I could make if I focused on growing to the next level during those hours.

Become more mindful of your use of time. *Do the math* every time, and you'll find out *what you are wasting valuable time on*. Remember, *time is the only asset that you cannot get more of*. The Bible tells us, "Teach us to number our days that we may apply our hearts to wisdom" (Psalm 90:12 KJV). We must learn to understand time so that we may be wise about how we invest or spend it.

Thirdly, is the one that has created the most grief and frustration for me: *Spend the time hiring the right people*.

Proverbs 26:10 (NIV) says, "An employer who hires a fool or a bystander is like an archer who shoots at random."

Invest the time to hire the right people. Properly vet them for *character, chemistry, capacity, and commitment*. Try your best to not hire to the pain but to the plan. Sometimes *we become so desperate to hire someone that we hire anyone*. That decision ends up doing much damage in the long term. One statistic said that making a bad hire can cost as much as $200,000. That is too expensive not to get it right.

Reflection

1. Quick Summary

2. Key Insights

3. Personal Application

4. Meaningful Quotes

WEEK 2

Gifts and Calling

I'm fascinated by people's tendency to view leaders as über-confident and graced with God-like abilities. They have no idea of the struggle with insecurity many leaders face. "*Am I doing what God has asked me to do?*" "*Am I really called for this?*" "*If I was genuinely called for this, why does it seem so difficult?*"

Whether in business or ministry, it is often difficult to know and understand what God is doing in a particular season. If we are not careful, we can become fraught with the insecurities and frailties of who we are in relation to what we are called to do. Confidence is certainly key. We have no confidence in the flesh, but as the Bible tells us, we put our confidence in Jesus, who is, in fact, the author and the finisher of our faith.

Romans 11:29 tells us that "the *gifts* and *calling* of God are without repentance."

Notice "gifts" is plural, and "calling" is singular.

The first thing we must recognize is that our calling is, in fact, from God—whether to marketplace ministry (or, in other words, business) or the Five-fold ministry. The verse also tells us that gifts accompany our calling. These gifts are divine enablement to accomplish all that God has called us to do.

He then tells us that the gifts and calling are without repentance—in other words, He doesn't take them back.

That's good news. It means that even though you have made and will make mistakes, His calling is still sure, and His purpose still reigns supreme. God operates in eternity, so He knows what you were going to go through before you did it. Yet He still called you. He knew the challenges you were going to have, yet He called you anyway.

And if He called you, then He also gifted you. If you are not careful, the pains and disappointments will begin to cause you to forget that you were gifted for such a time as this—that your calling and gifts are forever settled in eternity.

Remember, Romans 11:29 tells us that the gifts and calling of God are without repentance.

Notice the gifts come before the calling. They are in chronological order, because to do what God has called you to, you will need the gifts. Just because you can't emotionally discern or "feel" the gifts doesn't mean they are not there. When Samson jumped up from lying in Delilah's lap, he thought he could fight off the Philistines (Judges 16:19-21). If he could have felt the anointing, he would have known that the anointing wasn't there. Feelings are never an indication of gifting. If you want to know your giftings, then seek to understand your calling. And vice versa, if you are unsure what your calling is, seek to get clarity on your giftings. They go hand and hand and are used to interpret one another.

Just remember, gifts are like fruit; they must be developed. Every tree has fruit, but not every tree *has* fruit. What do I mean by that? Every tree has *the potential* of bearing fruit, but not every tree produces the same amount of fruit, and, in some cases, it bears none at all. Potential must never be confused with performance. Preparation time is never wasted time. I've observed people who have tried to step out into ministry before their time on the tree—it's tragic. They cite the urgency of ministry as if God is unaware of the time and season He brought them into.

I repeat: Preparation time is never wasted time. You must invest in your gifts to walk in your calling. People often see someone doing what they are called to do, and it looks easy, like the proverbial fish taking to water. That person has found the congruency and alignment that occurs when their gifts and calling line up.

You might say, "Well, I am not sure about either." Know this (and I promise you if you understand this, it will change everything): No matter what your calling is, it will require you to be proficient in the Word of God. If you are not already in a good, Bible-believing church, get into one. You cannot know the will of God with limited or skewed knowledge of the Word of God.

I have heard some people say, "If I am to be a prophet, I can only follow a prophet." While there is some truth to that—and of course, you should follow whomever God called you to follow—the best criterion for a spiritual leader is skill in the Word. That, ultimately, is the foundation of everything.

Finally, remember your gifts will make room for you, and self-realization is a lost art in today's society. Your gifts will open doors for you and bring you before great men. The Bible says that skilled or gifted men will stand before kings and not men of low rank (Proverbs 18:16). Not someone else's gifts, but *yours*.

Don't compare gifts. Be careful not to covet someone else's gift. The Bible warns that those who compare themselves among themselves are not wise (2 Cor. 10:12). Your gift is unique and special, and it is not less than or inferior to someone else's. The key is to find what you are gifted in and work out of that base.

Furthermore, remember that many will try to duplicate and imitate your gift, but *only you can truly be you*. So never worry about the copycats. They reminded me of the ERTL toy trucks I had when I was a kid. They are just like the real thing only smaller.

In 1998, Pfizer was developing a cardiovascular drug that failed miserably in clinical trials. The results were dismal at best. During testing, male volunteers were embarrassed to find themselves with an unusual side effect after taking the medication—they were "harder, firmer and lasted longer" than in their prior experience. A whole new market opened up for the little blue pill—drug UK92480 suddenly became Viagra, the fastest-selling drug of all time.[1]

---

[1] *FDA Approves Viagra*. 24 Nov. 2009, www.history.com/this-day-in-history/fda-approves-viagra.

Just because you may not have done so well at one thing does mean you will not excel at another. Invest the time to uncover what you're good at and do that. A famous quote says, "Everybody is a genius. but if you judge a fish by its ability to climb a tree, it will live its whole life believing that it is stupid." You are greater than you know. Go and be great!

Reflection

1. Quick Summary

2. Key Insights

3. Personal Application

4. Meaningful Quotes

WEEK 3

Knowing Your Worth

Years ago, after having been ousted from his own company (Apple computers), Steve Jobs started a company called NeXT. Needing to develop a logo and a brand, he contracted the 71-year-old no-nonsense designer Paul Rand for $100,000 to tackle the project. That must have been one heck of a logo.

Jobs said, "I asked Paul if he would come up with a few options, and he said, 'No, I will solve your problem for you. And you will pay me.'"[2] Wow, really.

But that in itself is the essence of all business and the source code for vision. Someone has a problem and will pay you to solve it. The vision and mission of your organization must be centered on understanding the problem and how you provide the right solution. I have heard it said that you are paid at the level of the problems you can solve.

Einstein summed it up best when he espoused that we cannot solve our problems with the same level of thinking that created them.[3]

If you are not prospering, then you need to find a more significant problem to solve. It sounds too easy, but it is really that simple.

A wealthy businessman was having lunch at a restaurant when he got a fishbone stuck in his throat and began choking. Fortunately, a doctor enjoying his sandwich at a nearby table knew exactly what to do. The doctor sprang up and told the businessman to take a few large bites of his sandwich. The bread dislodged the bone and saved the businessman's life.

As soon as the fellow had calmed himself and could talk again, he thanked the surgeon enthusiastically and offered to pay him, or at least pay for his lunch.

"Just name it," he croaked gratefully.

"Okay," replied the doctor. "How about half of what you would have offered when the bone was still stuck in your throat?"

"Do you see any truly competent workers? They will serve kings rather than working for ordinary people" (Proverbs 22:29 NLT).

---

[2] Popova, Maria. *Steve Jobs on Working with Legendary Designer Paul Rand*. 16 Oct. 2016, www.brainpickings.org/2010/01/05/steve-jobs-on-paul-rand/.

[3] Marc Prensky, Marc, and Albert Einstein. *The Problems That Exist in the World Today Cannot Be Solved by the Level of Thinking That Created Them*. citeseerx.ist.psu.edu/viewdoc/summary?doi=10.1.1.186.4598.

The Message (MSG) puts it this way: "Observe people who are good at their work—skilled workers are always in demand and admired; they don't take a backseat to anyone."

Often, people want to be known first, then do something great. But the reality is there is a thin line between famous and infamous. If you are great, it is inevitable that eventually, you will be known. Seek to be the best, be great at what you do, and I assure you, you will be known. Unfortunately, when you seek to be known first, you lose much time and expend effort trying to get to a place where your character and skill can't keep you.

I like to say it this way: "The anointing will open doors for you, but your character will keep you there."

Here's another one: "Giving a gift can open doors; it gives access to important people" (Proverbs 18:16 NLT).

I don't intend to minimize the other important skills required to be successful; however, I can tell you this. If you seek to solve a valuable problem and do it well, the rest has a way of working itself out—if you faint not!

Reflection

1. Quick Summary

2. Key Insights

3. Personal Application

4. Meaningful Quotes

WEEK 4

Portable Vision for Clarity

One of the most important jobs of a leader is to be the CCO. The Chief Clarity Officer. It is the most difficult thing to do, but I assure you, it is necessary and will clear up a lot of organizational friction. Clarity leaks, so bringing and protecting clarity continually must become a focused habit. Ministry and business always drift toward complexity.

Clarity is always leaking. In a car, three systems are predominately essential for its operation. They are fuel, lubrication, and power or spark. Without any one of these things, the car will not budge. It could be rusted out and still run if all of these three components are intact.

In your business or ministry, the driving force is *clarity*.

Clarity does three things:

It is the *fuel that provides momentum*, and it's the *oil that reduces friction* for long-term sustainable movement, eases the *friction* points, the *tension* spots, or, we could say, the *rub* they cause.

Finally, clarity is the *spark*. Once everyone clearly knows where you and they are going, it allows them to focus all their energy on being creative about how to get there.

Do your people know where you are going (*vision*), and do they know how you are going to get there (*mission*)?

Let's do a quick demonstration: Take out a blank piece of paper. No, really. Get a piece of paper. In the lower left-hand corner, draw a dot and write the word "here." In the upper right-hand corner, draw another dot and write the word "there." Now simply draw a line from the dot in the bottom left to the dot in the upper right and write "Mission" above that line. Then write "Core Values" below that line.

To clarify (pun intended), "here" is *where you are*, and "there" is the *vision of where you want to go*. How to get from "here" to "there" is the *mission*. Your *core values* are the guiding principles you adhere to as you *execute the mission to accomplish the vision*.

Creating a compelling vision is more important than people realize. Most people want to subscribe to the "build a better mousetrap" idea—if you build a better mousetrap, the world will beat a path to your door. Or as the famous line from the movie *Field of Dreams* goes, "If you build it, they will come."[4]

---

[4] Robinson, Phil Alden, director. *Field of Dreams*. Swank, 1989.

Unfortunately, in today's world, that is simply not true. You must be clear about what that field is and what it does. People have to know you've built a mousetrap and, more importantly, why it is better. And, specifically, *WIFM*—"What's In It For Me." Ergo marketing.

Years ago, Betamax and VHS went head to head to capture the home-movie-viewing marketplace. While Beta was a better format, they lost the marketing war. It didn't matter which was better; what mattered was who clearly demonstrated their value to the consumer.[5]

You may say, "I already have a clear mission and vision statement." You may even have your core values defined. But is your team at any moment and on cue able to recite it from memory? Or do they have to find it buried in the back of your handbook?

The vision must be characterized by what I call "the 3 Cs": *Clear*, *Concise*, and able to be *Carried* (or, in other words, *portable*), thereby creating a compelling Why.

Do you have a vision and a list of core values?

How many core values do you have?

Jim Collins, the author of *Good to Great* and *Built to Last*, said, "If you have more than three priorities, you don't have any."[6]

People often have extremely verbose visions and missions. Honestly, in ministry, they are harder to define concisely because of the self-imposed pressure to be theologically complete. Notice that I said theologically *complete*. We should always be theologically *sound*. The problem is you cannot be theologically *complete*—ever! There is not enough time for that, especially in a few sentences. For the most part, no one person has it all anyway.

The important part is for people to know *what you do*, *why*, and, more importantly, *what is in it for them*.

For example, one church's vision says the following:

Our vision is to become a biblically rooted and culturally sensitive church moved by a Great Commission Vision, which equips and enables men and women to communicate Christ through significant relationships with God, with one another as believers, and with non-believers. Our vision is to see God mature us into a local community of believers committed to serving those within the community of believers and seeking those outside the community of believers, both locally and globally, with character, compassion, courage, and creativity.

What they are really saying is, "We are demonstrating Christ by serving those around us."

---

[5] Wikipedia contributors. "Videotape format war." *Wikipedia, The Free Encyclopedia*. Wikipedia, The Free Encyclopedia, 13 Jul. 2020. Web. 22 Jul. 2020.

[6] Collins, James Charles. *Good to Great: Why Some Companies Make the Leap ... and Others Don't*. HarperBusiness, 2006.

With three billion dollars in revenue, The Ritz Carlton's vision statement is, "The Ritz-Carlton inspires life's most meaningful journeys."[7]

Their credo is "We are Ladies and Gentlemen serving Ladies and Gentlemen."[8]

It is Concise, Clear, and Carry-able (or portable). They let their employees know that they are ladies and gentlemen (so act that way) and that their guests are ladies and gentlemen, so treat them as you would like to be treated. Or love them as you love yourself. (Do you see what I did there?)

Jesus was clear regarding His mission in John 10:10. He said, "I came that they may have life." One translation says that they may have and ENJOY life.

Sometimes, people spend an inordinate amount of time making the simple overcomplicated. Give your team a compelling *why* and watch what happens. This is not the time to be cute or kitschy. Make it Clear, Concise, and Carry-able.

In the book of Habakkuk, the LORD tells the prophet, "Write the vision and make it plain so those that read it may run with it" (Habakkuk 2:2). In other words, make it clear and concise, and those that run may carry it. Notice he said "run" not "walk." The faster you want your organization to go, the clearer these things must be.

So make it Clear, Concise, and Carry-able. Then repeat it until everyone is sick of hearing it, including you.

I've heard a former US president quoted as saying, "I repeat myself until I am sick of saying it, then I know my staff has heard it for the first time. I keep repeating myself until my staff is tired of hearing it. When my staff is tired of hearing it, I know the Press Core has heard it for the first time. I continue repeating myself until the Press Core is tired of hearing it, and then I know the general public has heard it for the first time."

Political commentator David Gergen, a world-renowned expert on the subject of effectively communicating key messages, wrote in his New York Times bestseller *Eyewitness to Power: The Essence of Leadership Nixon to Clinton*, "History teaches that almost nothing a leader says is heard if spoken only once."[9]

There is an alignment that comes when everyone is on the same bus, and they become clear about the vision (where we are going), the mission (what are we doing to get there), and the core values (what guides our decisions and behaviors as we move towards the vision).

---

[7] *Luxury Hotels & Resorts: The Ritz.* www.ritzcarlton.com/en/about.

[8] *Luxury Hotels & Resorts: The Ritz.* www.ritzcarlton.com/en/about/gold-standards.

[9] Gergen, David. *EyeWitness To Power:The Essence of Leadership.* Simon & Schuster., 2000

Reflection

1. Quick Summary

2. Key Insights

3. Personal Application

4. Meaningful Quotes

WEEK 5

Obstacle, or Opportunity?

In the early '80s, Sir Richard Branson was stranded at an airport when his flight to the Virgin Islands was canceled. As it would for many of us, this delay created an immense amount of frustration and anger. So Branson chartered his own plane. He gave the charter company his credit card, hoping that it wouldn't get declined, and it actually went through. He then stood in the terminal with a chalkboard sign advertising "Virgin Airlines one-way: $39 to the Virgin Islands." The tickets immediately sold out, and voilà! A business opportunity was spawned.

As the passengers deplaned at their destination, one of them told Sir Richard that if he tightened up his service, he could really make a go of this airline!

The next day, he reached out to Boeing to see if they had any older planes they would sell him, and the rest, as they say, is history. Today, Virgin Airlines is the second-largest carrier in the UK.[10]

There are a few points here worth sharing with you.

    1. If you allow frustration and anger to cloud your judgment, you will miss the opportunity that could be right in front of you. Every obstacle is an opportunity for the person who sees it for what it is. There are always market inefficiencies that go beyond the normal scope of business. We must train ourselves to recognize them. It isn't always what you see directly in front of you. Sometimes you may have to step outside your comfort zone.

    2. Sir Richard dared to challenge the status quo. Chartering his own plane at the moment was a pretty brazen move. Many of us would have thought, "Start an airline? No way! Charter a plane? Who does that?" *Realizing that you serve a God who can do more than we could ask or think* is crucial. *Having the ability to dare to dream and know that anything is possible to them who believe* is absolutely necessary. *Removing the limitations of your negative self-talk* will allow you to step out into uncharted territory. Sir Richard wasn't sure he had enough credit on his card to afford chartering a plane. Sometimes your dream will cost more than you think you have. I am not saying to go out and empty your bank accounts; however, I am telling you never to let money keep you from starting the next great airline. There are many ways to finance your future. Get resourceful, and you will be surprised by what can be accomplished.

---

[10] Kachroo-Levine, Maya. *The Incredible Reason Why Richard Branson Started Virgin Atlantic.* 12 July 2019, www.travelandleisure.com/travel-tips/celebrity-travel/how-richard-branson-started-virgin-atlantic.

3. Make the call. Many years ago, I worked with someone who would always say to me, "You never know, just make the call." Many of us would have been afraid to call Boeing, the world's largest aerospace company. Sometimes you have to dare to make the call or send the email. The worst thing that can happen is the person at the other end, says no. Never forget there really is nowhere to go but up. As leaders, we are the ones who take calculated risks. You will always struggle if you are afraid of a no. Every no gets you statistically closer to a yes. Keep pushing, my friend, and you shall taste and see that the Lord is good.

4. Many a business has closed its doors because it failed to understand the viewpoint of its customers and to understand the frustration they experience. You must understand your customer from their perspective and have a true desire to rectify their problems and meet their needs. The most successful of businesses are always rooted in the customer's needs, not the business model. Sir Richard had a genuine desire never to see anyone stranded like that again, and hence a business was born.

There are many other lessons to learn from this story, but I will end on this note. Virgin Airlines became such a threat that British Airways gained access to their client records and started calling their clients, getting them to switch airlines by lying and telling them their flights had been canceled. It is amazing what a threat this small airline that started almost as a whim had become.

Virgin sued British Airways and subsequently won a million-dollar lawsuit against them because of their unscrupulous ways. Sir Richard took the million-dollar windfall and distributed it equally among the Virgin Airlines team.[11] It is not hard to rally your employees for the cause when you, as a leader, are willing to do things like that.

---

[11] Leasca, Stacey. *How Richard Branson Celebrated Virgin's Victory Over British Airways*. 14 Aug. 2017, www.travelandleisure.com/airlines-airports/virgin-america/richard-branson-virgin-british-airways-lawsuit

Reflection

1. Quick Summary

2. Key Insights

3. Personal Application

4. Meaningful Quotes

WEEK 6

Rinse and Repeat

"Lather, rinse, and repeat" is a common phrase seen in the instructions on shampoo bottles. Initially, I thought it was a ploy to get consumers to burn through shampoo and increase the frequency of repeat purchases.

A few years back, I watched my wife wash her hair, and she used the shampoo twice. I inquired why, and she told me that the first shampooing only took off the first layer of dirt and oil and that it was the second washing that really shampoos hair. As every man would be, I was somewhat skeptical, but I tried it later. She was pretty spot on, and I was shocked at how much lather was created by the second washing. After some research, I learned that the second wash would allow the shampoo's all-important ingredients to get to work, nourishing the strands and absorbing into the follicles.

Now I always rinse and repeat to keep these Samson-like locks of hair gleaming and healthy. Haha, I'm just teasing. But really, I learned something when it comes to *rinsing and repeating*. Oftentimes, we read an article, attend a training event, or even watch, let's say, my Monday morning "Master's Mind" videos. You may only watch it once. The reason why we only do one big idea a week is for you to do a deep dive into not only the principle but also the application of it. We give you the entire week to watch it over and over it until you have mined every nugget and kernel of revelation and help from it. Statistically, *we retain only 20 percent of what we see and hear the first time.*

This is the reason why marketing says that *a person needs to hear or see your message at least seven times before it is committed to memory.*[12] When we go through something only once, we only get a little bit of its whole content.

I have books and audiotaped messages that I have reread and listened to many times, and I learn so much more each time. Often the first time I listen or read something, I am just becoming familiar with the material, and I am focused only on the speaker or writer.

Information comes from a few places, and by listening only once, you are missing the depth of what I call *three-hundred-and-sixty-degree learning*, i.e., rinse and repeat.

Let me explain. Frequently, on my first pass through the material I'm reading or hearing, I focus on just getting through it. But I notice that the more I repeat going

---

[12] *Marketing Fundamentals: The Rule of 7.* 14 Oct. 2019, siglcreative.com/2019/06/07/rule-of-7/.

through the information, the more inspiration and ideas will come to me from other sources as well.

Think of it this way: When I first listen to or read the material, I am just starting to get it into me. If I can only absorb approximately 20 percent at a time, it could potentially take a few times through before I internalize it all. Then inspiration comes from the environment around me. Once I have it in me, then I begin to see patterns and references in other things around me like movies, conversations, other learning materials, or life in general. Then finally, as I continue to review the material again, God will speak thoughts and ideas that I can write down. The total growth comes from 360 degrees. In other words, it comes from within. It comes from around. Then it comes from above.

There is a term called *the Baader-Meinhof Phenomenon*. Have you ever bought a car and noticed after you purchased it, it seems like everybody in the world bought one too? You start seeing it everywhere. Well, that is called the Baader-Meinhof Phenomenon; you are only more aware of it because you now have one.[13] Surely you do not believe that everyone went and bought that same car when you decided to buy one!

Romans 10:17 says that "faith cometh by hearing and hearing by the word of God." See, faith doesn't come by what you heard. It comes by *hearing*, the *active* part of the repetition.

"Rinse and repeat" causes you to take a deep dive into the information and get all you can out of it. "Rinse and repeat" is sometimes also used as a humorous way of saying that a certain set of instructions should be repeated until an explicit or implicit goal is reached. While the term may be used in jest, it implies an immense amount of truth. Studying a wide range of subjects is like beginning to drill a bunch of shallow holes instead of sticking with a few holes that you drill deep till you strike oil.

1 Corinthians 4:15 says you can have many teachers, and the Amplified translation says you will have only a few who will take responsibility for you. Sometimes we have to recognize that we don't need everybody and everything, but we need those who are specific and focused on helping us. There is a difference between just-in-case learning and just-in-time learning. Unless you're studying for personal enjoyment, study things that are going to help you now—not someday!

Many of us tend to go wide and consume as much information as possible when we need to focus on going deep. Focus on the few, master those, and don't try to be a jack of all trades and a master of none. Bruce Lee said, "I don't fear a man who has practiced ten thousand kicks." He said he fears the man who has practiced *one kick ten thousand times*.

---

[13] Pietrangelo, Ann. *Understanding the Baader-Meinhof Phenomenon*. 17 Dec. 2019, www.healthline.com/health/baader-meinhof-phenomenon.

Reflection

1. Quick Summary

2. Key Insights

3. Personal Application

4. Meaningful Quotes

WEEK 7

Selling Sugar Water

In 1983, Steve Jobs approached John Sculley, then president of PepsiCo, and asked him to join Apple. Sculley made it clear that he was not interested. He was perplexed as to why Steve Jobs thought he would leave a large, established company like Pepsi for a four-year-old startup that began in a garage.

Then Jobs lowered the boom when He asked Sculley this famous question: "Do you want to sell sugar water for the rest of your life, or do you want to come with me and change the world?"[14]

Over half of today's marketplace consists of millennials. Truth be told, millennials are the subject of incessant griping due to their perceived laziness and lack of dedication. The truth is that every generation has felt that the generation following theirs were all going to hell with gasoline drawers on, including yours. Millennials don't lack work ethic. They don't lack commitment or passion. They lack a qualified leader.

In one of my favorite movies of all time, *Remember the Titans*, Julius Campbell and Gerry Bertier are on the football field. Gerry is reprimanding Julius for not being a team player, and he quips in response, "Attitude reflects leadership… Captain."[15]

Millennials need a compelling "why." At their core, most great people do. Millennials need it to be made a little clearer, and they need it to be clear upfront.

Gone are the days of people who will work for 20 years before they become clear about the impact they get to make. If they don't see meaning in what they do, they are "out of there."

All of us need a compelling reason why we do what we do. And it needs to be compelling to not only you but to others around you. If you are passionate about something and no one else is, then it is a hobby or a charitable cause, not your ministry or your business.

It was hard to believe that making and selling computers would change the world. I am sure it seemed dramatic in the '80s. But looking back over history, they have, in fact, done just that. Apple technology changed not only the computer world but also the handheld-tablet world and the cellular-phone world. And, in terms of music, not only did they redefine how we purchase music but also how we listen to it.

---

[14] Gallo, Carmine. "How Steve Jobs And Bill Gates Inspired John Sculley To Pursue The 'Noble Cause'." *Forbes*, 12 Nov. 2016, www.forbes.com/sites/carminegallo/2016/11/12/how-steve-jobs-and-bill-gates-inspired-john-sculley-to-pursue-the-noble-cause/#8a1b106232bd. Accessed 22 July 2020.

[15] Yakin, Boaz, director. *Remember the Titans*. Buena Vista Pictures, 2000.

You have to look deeper into what you do. For example, according to the world's definition, you may sell real estate, but in actuality, you broker the most significant transaction the average person makes; you protect their interest; you help them to build a home, a life, and a future. You mitigate shelter insecurities. You are one of the core backbones of the economy. When you say, "I just sell houses," you negate the true reality of what you do because it seems like a light thing to you. It has no power to give you the juice and keep you, nor anyone else, for that matter, motivated to continue through the thick and thin. In lean times, we are often reassessing our priorities. Truthfully, if you don't have a compelling reason "why" you do what you do, you will give up.

The reality is that Pepsi doesn't just sell sugar water; they contribute to the success of just about every eating experience, party, and event. They are a critical part of the entertainment.

If nothing else, Pepsi is a market maker for dentists. Did you know that, years ago, Alka-Seltzer created a spicy cookbook to help drive their sales? Alka-Seltzer is not important until it's important.

I am reminded of a story—

A giant ship engine failed. The ship's owners tried to repair the engine, hiring one expert after another, but none could figure out how.

Then they brought in an older man who had been fixing ships since he was young. He carried a large bag of tools with him. When he arrived, he immediately went to work. He inspected the engine very carefully, top to bottom.

Two of the ship's owners were there, watching this man, hoping he would know what to do. After looking things over, the old man reached into his bag and pulled out a small hammer. He gently tapped something. Instantly, the engine lurched into life. He carefully put his hammer away. The engine was fixed!

A week later, the owners received a bill from the old man for ten thousand dollars. "What?!" the owners exclaimed. "He hardly did anything!"

So they wrote the old man a note saying, "Please send us an itemized bill.

The man sent a bill that read:

Tapping with a hammer..................... $ 2.00
Knowing where to tap....................... $ 9,998.00

The effort is important, but knowing where to make an effort makes all the difference!

Spend some time getting clear about your *why*.

Highly skilled people usually can figure out *how* when they have a compelling enough *why*.

Reflection

1. Quick Summary

2. Key Insights

3. Personal Application

4. Meaningful Quotes

WEEK 8

The Tension of Being Unreasonable

Have you ever used a rubber band? It is one of the most effective tools a business leader can have, and I don't mean to hold stuff together. I will explain shortly.

I have often been told that I am unreasonable. I think people saying that may think they are hurting my feelings, but I know that one of the key traits of a visionary and leader is being, you guessed it, unreasonable! The Bible tells us that God "is able to do exceeding abundantly above all that we ask or think, according to the power that worketh in us" (Ephesians 3:20).

You must realize that the only one who can limit God is you.

It is the job of the leader to see what seems impossible and stretch toward it. Take the Wright brothers, for example. Orville Wright said, "Isn't it astonishing that all these secrets have been hidden for so many years just so we could uncover them?"[16]

Leaders must push toward the unbelievable. The impossible has to become so real in them that others will think they are unreasonable.

The world of possibilities awaits us all. So many secrets have been hidden for us; all we have to do is dare to believe.

The pantheon of success is dominated by unreasonable people. Vincent Van Gogh sold only one painting while he was alive and almost starved.[17] Beethoven composed five of the best-loved symphonies of all time, even when he was going deaf.[18] In 1936, no one believed that a runner could jump 26 feet, 5-3/8 inches. It had never been done for the first 35 years of the modern Olympics, but Jesse Owens did it, and his record stood for another 25 years.[19]

Honestly, nobody thinks a certain thing can be done until someone does it.

No one thought that minorities would enjoy the same civil rights as the majority until a man named Martin Luther King Jr. ransomed his life for the cause. Martin Luther King Jr. penned this from a Birmingham jail:

---

[16] Bellis, Mary. "Quotes of the Wright Brothers." ThoughtCo, Feb. 11, 2020, thoughtco.com/famous-quotes-of-the-wright-brothers-1992679.

[17] History.com Editors. "Vincent Van Gogh Chops off His Ear." *History*, 24 Nov. 2009, www.history.com/this-day-in-history/van-gogh-chops-off-ear. Accessed 23 July 2020.

[18] *20 Greatest Symphonies*. www.wned.org/radio/wned-classical-945/20-greatest-symphonies/.

[19] *Jesse Owens Jumps for Gold*. 9 July 2020, www.olympic.org/news/jesse-owens-jumps-for-gold.

"I must confess that I am not afraid of the word 'tension.' I have earnestly opposed violent tension, but there is a type of constructive, nonviolent tension which is necessary for growth. Just as Socrates felt that it was necessary to create a tension in the mind so that individuals could rise from the bondage of myths and half-truths to the unfettered realm of creative analysis and objective appraisal...."[20]

A rubber band is needed solely for the purpose of tension. It is the tension that gives the rubber band its purpose. When we stretch the rubber band, it causes tension. Most people do not like tension and tend to seek to resolve it immediately. We have a saying on our team: "Is it a problem to solve, or a tension to manage?"

Please catch this. Some situations cannot be solved; they must be managed. Great stress and pain have come from people trying to solve what needs to be managed. Not knowing the difference between the two can be a great source of frustration. Trying to manage what can be solved and trying to solve what should be managed can cause great pain. Tension, although uncomfortable, is a necessary part of organizational growth.

Imagine stretching a rubber band vertically—the top represents your vision as the leader. People at the top have the vision and are always pulling what's under them upward, stretching the boundaries of the possible and daring to "reach toward the mark," as the apostle Paul said in Philippians 3.

At the bottom of this rubber band are the realists. They tend to be more grounded and rooted in the current status quo and are, at times, viewed as unwilling to change because they are stuck in the mire of what has only been done before.

The tension is necessary for others to become clear about the path from the bottom to the top, which is the vision. As long as the leadership holds strong to the vision, the tension will cause the bottom to rise. Steve Jobs said it best: "There must always be someone who is the keeper of the vision. When the vision is held, it pulls everything up, and the organization is elevated."

Yet if the reality prevails, it then pulls the vision down. We must also bear in mind that if we ignore reality, it will eventually snap the band. We must manage the gentle working and coaxing of tension.

Additionally, we must understand that the vision is never fully accomplished. It must continue to stretch not only your team but also you.

The tension created is supposed to be energizing, and as Reverend King said, it is "necessary to create a tension in the mind so that individuals could rise from the bondage of myths and half-truths to the unfettered realm of creative analysis and objective appraisal...."

---

[20] "Socrates in Martin Luther King, Jr.'s 'A Letter from a Birmingham Jail.'" 18 Jan. 2010, iris.haverford.edu/2010/01/18/socrates-in-martin-luther-king-jr-s-a-letter-from-a-birmingham-jail/. Accessed 23 July 2020.

In other words, to accomplish what our minds deem impossible, you must harness the tension and leverage it for your success. You must confront the bondage of half-truths and the lies we tell ourselves to justify our complacency. You are not unreasonable; you're just a visionary. Stay with it, and you will see it come to pass.

Reflection

1. Quick Summary

2. Key Insights

3. Personal Application

4. Meaningful Quotes

WEEK 9

The Time I Almost Quit

Have you ever been so overwhelmed, so under pressure in ministry and in business that you've considered quitting?

Well, according to one study, approximately 1,500 pastors leave the ministry monthly, and 7,000 churches close annually.[21]

It happened to me about ten years ago, right after I launched our church. At that point, I had been in ministry for nearly five years. As an entrepreneur for close to 15 years, I was no stranger to busy seasons. But something happened, and I wasn't ready. After years of serving our church, where I had no team, no staff, and a TON of good ministry to do, my business was also suffering from a lack of attention.

The problem was it was too much for me—or at least that's what I thought!

I was miserable. It was the closest I ever came to quitting the ministry. I felt like I had no-one to turn. The people I knew who had the knowledge and experience to help me were, in my mind, too busy to help my small little ministry, and the people who were around and offered to help had agendas and motives that I was just too uncertain about. I thought that if I was truly anointed and called, then I should have all the answers.

After all, a minister should have all the answers, right?

On that day, I almost quit. Did you read that? I almost quit!

God began to deal with me about some key biblical principles of success. Remember, I was over-stressed and overwhelmed not because my load was too heavy, but because I didn't have the right tools and understanding to get it all done. I realized I needed to revamp my systems and organization to structure them for growth and not control. Contrary to popular belief, you cannot have both (which, by the way, is one of the principles I am going to share with you).

I made a few *simple adjustments*, and *my ministry and effectiveness changed seemingly overnight*. Recently I was thinking about that season, and I asked myself a question: If I were to take the 15 years of my experience and sum it up for anyone getting into ministry, what would I tell them to help them avoid the pitfalls and the potholes that I experienced?

The first thing I did was write down everything I had dealt with and how I got resourceful to resolve them. I just dumped it on paper. I expected that list to be a mile long—it was. Now, that list wasn't perfect. But it was the beginning of an idea.

---

[21] *Statistics for Pastors*, www.pastoralcareinc.com/statistics/.

From there, I examined that list for ways to reduce it to the minimum. I found trends and patterns to the problems I had experienced, and the common denominator was, ta-da! You guessed it—me.

That's when I discovered six principles that helped me overcome. This POWERFUL and FOCUSED list is a simple compilation of things that helped me, and it can help you, too, IF you know the secrets and how to apply them.

Relax. I am not selling anything. I am giving it away to you right now. So without further ado, let's get started.

The first thing I want to share, which I alluded to earlier is:

You must grow for your organization to grow.

I have pastored multiple churches and have only pastored one church. Growth means that you start with the proverbial "man in the mirror" when it comes to leadership. Your people are not the problem; it is you. It is a poor carpenter who blames his tools. We must, as leaders, realize that the buck truly stops with us. Often when we are frustrated with people in our ministries or our organizations, it is rooted in the fact that they *are trained to give you what you used to want and not what will be needed for where you are going.* You may find that you shouldn't have released the responsibility for certain areas, and will need to take them back. Most likely, you have not released enough to others to become responsible for the outcomes. You can structure your organization for control or growth, but not for both.

That means you may have to get up on the balcony, stop working *in* the business, and start working *on* the business to see where you need to go. Then, staff and train to your *destination* and not according to your *journey*.

Use only tithers in leadership positions.

While this may seem more ministry-related, it applies in business as well. *Tithing is not just your money but also your time, treasure, and talent.* Never put people in leadership who are stingy with their time, talent, and treasure. If they are the last one in and the first to leave, they're stingy with giving of their time. If they are unwilling to spring for an occasional lunch or coffee, they are stingy with their money and not qualified for leadership.

People often hire to *pain* as opposed to hiring to *plan* because they need help. As tempting as it may be, the Bible says in Proverbs 26:10, "An employer who hires a fool or a bystander is like an archer who shoots at random."

We must be purposeful in choosing the right leaders to carry the vision.

Run to the battles.

"As the Philistine moved closer to attack him, David ran quickly toward the battle line to meet him" (1 Samuel 17:48–50, NIV).

Making difficult discussions is what we, as leaders, do. I struggled with this, and I learned to follow a few rules.

1. Script it. Take the time to write down your key points.

2. Honor the person you're speaking to. Assume the best of them and that they want to change.

3. Set clear outcomes, expectations, and next steps.

Remember, ministers, preaching on it is *not* the same as confronting the issue. And ultimately, as a leader, you have to be *slow to hire and quick to fire*.

Reflection

1. Quick Summary

2. Key Insights

3. Personal Application

4. Meaningful Quotes

WEEK 10

The Time I Almost Quit - Part 2

Don't do it!
And whosoever doth not bear his cross and come after me cannot be my disciple. For which of you, intending to build a tower, sitteth not down first, and counteth the cost, whether he have sufficient to finish it? Lest haply, after he hath laid the foundation, and is not able to finish it, all that behold it begin to mock him, Saying, This man began to build and was not able to finish (Luke 14:27–30).

If you can do anything else, then do it. If you can find the strength, desire, and/or ability to do anything else, then do just that. The ministry world and the business world are already full of tire kickers. Jeremiah said it was shut up in his bones like a fire (Jer. 20:9). If you can do anything else, then do it. But if it is in you to such a degree that you can't do anything else, then do it now and be certain you have counted the cost.

What does it take to do big things for God? Only EVERYTHING!

Learn the Art of "NO."
"So teach us to number our days, that we may apply our hearts unto wisdom" (Psalms 90:12).

Warren Buffet once said, "The difference between successful people and really successful people is that really successful people say no to almost everything."[22] Since, by nature, humans try and please everyone, you have to start out with an independence of mind to know that you cannot please everyone. You must be focused, and that means you have to say NO. This two-letter word is one of the greatest time management tools known to man. While the promises of God are yes and amen, you are not God and must know the art of NO. In my own life, I often find that if I can't say "heck yeah!" then the answer is a "heck NO!"

One of the best tools I've found is called "The Art of The NO Sandwich." Whenever you have to tell someone no, package it between two positive things so that it is not such a difficult pill for them to swallow. For example, sometimes my assistant will have to say no to a meeting request on my behalf. Her response will be something to this effect: "I know Dr. Gene really wants to meet with you. However, at this moment, his schedule doesn't permit that. He wanted me to respond to you personally, and thank you for the invite."

---

[22] Blaschka, Amy. "This Is Why Saying 'No' Is The Best Way To Grow Your Career—And How To Do It." *Forbes*, 26 Nov. 2019, www.forbes.com/sites/amyblaschka/2019/11/26/this-is-why-saying-no-is-the-best-way-to-grow-your-career-and-how-to-do-it/#244e44d3479d. Accessed 23 July 2020.

It is "Yes-No-Yes," all packaged up in a sandwich.

Last but not least—

Take Care of Yourself and feed the flock of God.

Protect your family time and life balance.

"Then, because so many people were coming and going that they did not even have a chance to eat, he said to them, 'Come with me by yourselves to a quiet place'" (Mark 6:31 NIV).

Often, the demands of business or ministry can pull us off-center and cause us to become unbalanced. Kenneth Hagin Sr. used to say, "Develop a morning and night routine of rest, rejuvenation, hydration and nourishment because anything that is unbalanced will get off into error."

After his death, Martin Luther King's Jr. autopsy found that while he was just 39 years old, he had the heart of a 60-year-old. Doctors concluded that the pressure he experienced during his career had stressed and aged his heart.[23]

One reason why major insurance companies require what's called "key man insurance" for businesses is because they are uniquely aware that a business relies on its founder and principal more than most people are aware. And they must insure themselves in case anything happens to that person.

Life is a marathon, not a sprint. Please be mindful of taking care of yourself and knowing your boundaries. Love your personal time, your spouse, love on your kids, take a vacation, and as Joyce Meyer would say, "buy the shoes and eat the cookie." The new buzz word is "self-care." Don't allow Satan to spin you out like a top. We must finish the race set before us.

Alright, so here is a bonus—a baker's dozen, so to speak.

Don't go it alone. Get a confidante.

"Where no counsel is, the people fall: but in the multitude of counselors, there is safety" (Proverbs 11:14).

Be quick to find someone you can connect to. In one of his award acceptance speeches, recording artist Prince said, "A mentor or a good friend is never on your payroll." Take the time to connect with someone who will do three things for you: 1) Develop your gift, 2) Disturb your complacency, and 3) Help you design your life.

We all need somebody to believe in us.

---

[23] "Citizen King'". *American Experience*. PBS. Retrieved July 23, 2020.

Reflection

1. Quick Summary

2. Key Insights

3. Personal Application

4. Meaningful Quotes

WEEK 11

They Laughed @ Me

When I was 18 years old, I wrote my first business plan for an optical business. I was working part-time in an optical store filing records, one of my first jobs in high school. One day, one of the opticians quit and walked out. In an extremely frustrated state, the manager turned to me and asked if I wanted to learn how to be an optician. To which I replied, "Y-yes, Ma'am!" I then began to learn the business and eventually learned the ins and outs of its operation. I decided that a business with an almost 500% margin was one I wanted to own and not just work for. At 18, I began to write my business plan.

I spent weeks perfecting it, assembling all the data and pro forma calculations. Finally, it was ready. I scouted locations, studied traffic patterns, and found the perfect mall to place it in. I knew it would be a moneymaker and that I was on to something. I had only one problem—a lack of money.

I did some research and started calling venture capital and angel investors until I found someone who would take an appointment with me. I prepared my complete presentation on transparencies (that should tell you how long ago this was). I invested in a projector and went to pitch my million-dollar business idea. When I arrived at their very intimidating office, I was determined that they would love the idea as much as I did and throw cash my way to make it happen. Overcoming all my butterflies and nerves, I set up my overhead projector and pitched my idea. The angel investor listened intently and even took notes. Inside, I was thinking, "Got 'em!"

After my presentation, the investor asked me a load of questions and then thanked me for my time and said he would get back to me—the universal brush-off; the old "Don't call me, I'll call you."

I was crushed...

...until one day, I happened to be driving past the location where I had intended to place my optical store. Lo and behold, there was a new optical store. After some research, I figured out that my potential investor and taken my idea and implemented it. But without me.

I realized then that I'd thought it was a bad idea and that *maybe* I had missed it because of their rejection. Truthfully, it was a great idea—great enough for them to steal it from me. I never understood until later that all the while, God was protecting me from being in business with people who would steal from me. The Bible tells us that no weapon formed against us will prosper (Isaiah 54:17). Many forget that we don't recognize all the weapons God will shut down for our sake.

I learned a few lessons from this experience:

1) Never share your ideas with people who have not signed a non-disclosure agreement.

2) God will always protect His children from harm even when they don't know it. And finally, (this is the one I want to unpack a little)—

3) Have a business plan so clear that your enemy could pick it up and do what you do.

The Bible says to write the vision and make it plain (Habakkuk 2:2). This is often overlooked. Even if you've started your businesses already, take the time to write out your business plan. Get clear about what you do and how you do it. You will be shocked at the revelations and understanding that will come as you gain clarity about the what, the why, and the how.

Reflection

1. Quick Summary

2. Key Insights

3. Personal Application

4. Meaningful Quotes

WEEK 12

6 Questions to Refocus

Times come in every leader's life when they must recalibrate and refocus. Let's face it, life tends to drift toward complexity. I am not talking about going out and buying a mid-life crisis Harley or Ferrari (although buying either one, whether mid-life or not, is not altogether a bad idea— But I digress). I am talking about the pain of *autopilot*. Sometimes we become so busy working "in" life that we forget to work "on" life. Our plan or design for our life has to be re-centered. Even precision instruments or a piano or a computer will have to be recalibrated occasionally— unless you own a Mac, of course.

Sometimes you have to ask yourself the difficult questions and realize that *you* are worth the effort of getting up on the balcony. You need to see further down the road and start working on your life and not just in it.

Thinking is very underrated nowadays in a society that tries to wrest control from you and influence every area of your life.

I am reminded of a story about Henry Ford. One day, he was interviewed by a reporter. As the reporter was led down the hallway to Ford's office, he walked past one of Ford's employees. The man was sitting in his office with his feet up on the desk, chewing on a pencil and gazing intently out the window.

When the interview concluded, as Ford walked him to the door, the reporter again noticed this individual still sitting at his desk with his feet up, staring out the window. Having just interviewed a man who modernized and revolutionized the automotive industry by creating highly efficient and organized work systems, the perplexed reporter asked why this man appeared to be doing nothing but staring out a window.

Ford replied, "He is thinking, and that is what I pay him to do."

Be mindful of maintaining margin, or think time, in your schedule, and treat it as an appointment with the president. I am often blown away when I see people who are dressed up in pictures when they meet someone important, yet they don't think it important to dress well for themselves. They value others more than they value themselves. My best-dressed days will not be spent in a casket.

My point is you are worth making an appointment with yourself and keeping it. Don't cancel or move it because "something more important came along." There is nothing more important than designing *you*.

I have compiled six questions to ask yourself as a helpful assessment tool. Remember, Psalms 90:12: "Teach us to number our days that we may apply our hearts to wisdom." Experience doesn't make us better; evaluated experience does.

Maybe you can get away for a quiet weekend somewhere, find a local coffee shop, or sit down with your spouse or a close friend, and consider the following questions to refocus and build *You 2.0*:

1. What are the recurring themes in your life that God seems to be dealing with?

In seasons of life, some overall themes will encompass our study, devotional time, and prayers. What is that theme for you right now? Invest the time to find out.

The Bible says that it is the glory of God to conceal a matter, but it is the honor of kings to search it out (Proverbs 25:2). I have heard many people say God never speaks to them, but I disagree. Often, those recurring themes in people's lives are God speaking to them and leading them where He wants them to go.

Once you begin to develop that understanding, pray it through with God, spend time just asking, and, more importantly, listen. One of the most fatal mistakes is when people pray, hang up the phone, and never wait or listen long enough to hear God's answer. Be still and know that He is God, and you will be surprised how much He will reveal to you.

2. What is my single greatest strength? (What do I "do" the best?) Often this question trips people up because, for leaders, this becomes multi-pronged:

    a. What is the most important thing I can do to grow the ministry and/or my company?

    b. What is the most important thing I do to "make it rain"?

    c. What am I really good at?

Understanding that what you're good at may not *exactly* be what makes the most impact on the business or ministry. However, you need to know *what* those things are, seek to *understand* how they interact and affect each other and begin to *invest* in your development for those things. If you are terrible at accounting, don't spend a bunch of money and time trying to figure out the numbers on the spreadsheets. Spend time and money on the key things that you are good at to become GREAT at them. Pay a professional to count the beans.

A word of caution, though. Never let go of the checkbook, meaning don't blindly allow anyone to control the purse strings without you being intimately hands-in (and "hands-in" is not the same as "hands-on").

3. What three decisions are causing me the greatest stress? Ask yourself, "What is causing my greatest anxiety?"

Mark Twain said, "Eat the frog first, and nothing worse can happen to you for the rest of the day." Sometimes you have to jump into the pool despite the cold water. The tippy-toe approach delays the pain and causes more emotional anguish than your problems deserve. Your emotions should be spent on being resourceful and solving problems, not dreading them.

Have you ever seen a cow sitting in the field, looking like it's chewing bubble gum? Cows have multiple compartments to their stomachs. In order to process and break down the grass they eat, they will swallow the grass, bring it back up to chew it again, and ingest it into the next part of their stomach.[24] You are not a cow; chew it once and be done with it.

4. What should I quit?

Peter Drucker said, "Efficiency is doing things right; effectiveness is doing the right things." What things are on your plate that someone else can do at least half as well as you? The reason I say "half as well" is because, truthfully, your assessment of your ability to do things is probably over-inflated. If you ask yourself what tasks someone can do as well as you, oftentimes, the answer is nothing, and you are right back at square one. If someone can do something half as well as you, that's a good indication that it is time to give it over to them so you can do more of whatever you are good at or need to be good at.

Secondly, some things you may need to quit doing, period—not hand them off, but stop doing them altogether. These things have limited outcomes, and time and resources would be better spent elsewhere to produce a greater result. This is pruning the rose bush, so to speak.

5. What are the "maybes" on your calendar?

If something is not a resounding, *"Heck yeah!"* it should be a definite *"Heck no!"* If you want to grow and scale anything, you have to be delivered from the idea that other people run your calendar. Many people will think that, for various reasons, they deserve access to your schedule and time. The more successful you become, the more family, friends, and peers will find a way to be upset with you because you won't do this or that. Honestly, no matter what you do, it will never be enough anyway. They will be the first ones to hit you up for a loan when you make it to the big leagues, but complain all along the way when you are not available at their beck and call.

I am not telling you what I heard, I am telling you what I know. Warren Buffet said that really successful people say no to just about everything. Time is a zero-sum game, and I urge you to protect your time more than your money.

6. If money, time, or resources were not an issue, what three things could you do in the next 90 days to make a huge difference?

One of the biggest problems people face is the finite extent of their imagination. They limit themselves from dreaming as if they had no creativity to stretch. People often tell themselves, "Well, that's not possible because I don't know how. I don't have the resources."

The challenge is that, at one point, all innovation was impossible until someone did it. Air travel was impossible until the Wright brothers pushed the envelope of possibilities and dared to dream. We would not have any of our modern conveniences if someone didn't dare to dream. If we see all our dreams through the lens of our limitations, that lens becomes a limiting belief. With God, ALL things are possible to him that believes (Matthew 19:26). Do you know what "all" means in Hebrew or Greek? It means ALL! How about in Spanish? ALL!

---

[24] Linn, James, et al. "The Ruminant Digestive System." *University of Minnesota Extension*, 2018, Accessed 23 July 2020.

Dare to take off the blinders and see what could make the difference for you through the eyes of the One who has no limitations and not through the frailty of yourself.

Reflection

1. Quick Summary

2. Key Insights

3. Personal Application

4. Meaningful Quotes

WEEK 13

Champions Have Short Memory

At Wimbledon 2019, Novak Djokovic defeated Roger Federer in the finals of the world-renowned tennis tournament for the Gentlemen's Singles Championship. In the opening game of the first set, Federer initially looked like the clear winner and had what appeared to be a great lead. He eventually lost the first set. Plagued by unforced errors, Federer wound up beating himself, in my opinion. He appeared a little frustrated at the end of the first set. However, when he started the second set, by his excellence of play, he seemed unfazed and unaffected by his preceding performance. The commentator then made this statement that stuck with me: "Champions have short memories." Unfortunately for Federer, he eventually lost the overall final, in a match that became the longest final match in Wimbledon history at just under 5 hours.[25]

What stood out to me is the statement that "champions have short memories." Much of sports is centered on establishing and maintaining the proper mindset before an athlete has to perform.

When it comes to ministry, I hear people say things like, "Well, the anointing wasn't in the service today." That is an unbiblical concept. The truth is the gifts and calling are irrevocable. That means God can't and won't take them back. That means a ministry leader or pastor is equally anointed on a good day as on a bad day. I have learned that performance rises and falls based on focus and mindset. We are truly affected by the headspace we are in at the time.

Brethren, I count not myself to have apprehended: but this one thing I do, forgetting those things which are behind, and reaching forth unto those things which are before, I press toward the mark for the prize of the high calling of God in Christ Jesus (Philippians 3:13–14).

I think we have to recognize that there is a mentality that produces selective amnesia, and it is the ability to selectively forget failures and get back on the horse.

Failures tend to plague us all. As they say, hindsight is 20/20, and our past can often be the baggage that hinders our race. The apostle Paul said to lay aside the weight that so easily besets us so that we are not hindered in running our race. Your business or ministry, or even your career, can become tethered to the failures of your

---

[25] "Novak Djokovic vs Roger Federer | Wimbledon 2019 | Full Match." *YouTube,* uploaded by Wimbledon, 01 August 2019, www.youtube.com/watch?v=TUikJi0Qhhw.

past. It can become a weight that will slow you down in the best-case scenario, and in the worst-case scenario, stop you dead in your tracks.

You have to be careful of not only your failures but also your successes. Sometimes successfully handling something in a particular way can pigeonhole you into thinking that everything should be handled in that exact same way. To a hammer, everything is a nail. We have to be clear that God doesn't always do everything the same way every time. If you are not careful, you can condition yourself to believe and expect things always to be done the same way and ultimately miss the moving of God. Behold, He may be doing a new thing, and if you are not careful, you could miss it.

See, champions have to have short memories. You have to remember enough to remain confident and forget enough not to be influenced by mistakes from your last game.

Week 13: Champions Have Short Memory

Reflection

1. Quick Summary

2. Key Insights

3. Personal Application

4. Meaningful Quotes

WEEK 14

Change Your Environment

Dr. BJ Fogg, Director of the Behavior Design Lab at Stanford, said, "There's just one way to radically change your behavior: radically change your environment."[26]

Many people underestimate the value of how they feel. As people of faith, we don't walk by sight; we walk by faith, and we are taught that feelings are evil. But feelings are not evil. Unsanctified feelings, or feelings that are not submitted to God, are evil.

Philippians 4:8 tells us that we need to think on those things that are pure and lovely. Having our minds affected by good things is crucial to our overall success. We often underestimate the impact that a bad environment can have on us. We are creative beings, and we have to pay attention to our environment. A cluttered environment leads to a cluttered mind.

Guarding what you think on, I believe, includes creating an environment that fosters lovely things. It matters how your car looks when you drive to work. I believe it is honorable toward God to treat well the things you have. Someone who knew me very well got into my car one day and said it looked as new as the day I bought it even though I'd had it for years.

I think having nice things is important, and it helps my overall frame of mind. Your office should contain beautiful things (not so many that they distract you, but enough that they provide a comfortable environment for you as you work). You want a desk and comfortable chair that are conducive for you to do your best work. We often have our priorities backward. We sit in the most comfortable chair in the house to watch television, then wonder why we spend too much time watching television.

Creating an environment to be successful helps us to keep our minds stayed on what is important. People, by nature, are lazy. We all will take the paths of least resistance. I want to stress to you the importance of changing your environment to promote what you want to think and focus on.

If you are working on your health, dietary changes start with changing your environment. Put the healthy snacks within reach and the bad ones far away from you. Stop buying them altogether. Or buy a small bag of chips that will require you to go back to the store if you want more instead of buying a big family-size trough bag. Grocery stores and casinos use design to prompt and influence your buying decisions and behaviors. You need to learn to do the same.

---

[26] Fogg, B. J. *Tiny Habits: the Small Changes That Change Everything.* Thorndike Press, 2020.

Reduce friction on things you want to do and increase friction on things you don't want to do. In other words, make doing the things you want to do *lighter on yourself* and doing the things you want to stop doing *harder*.

If you want to eat less, buy smaller plates so that to eat more, you have to make more trips for refills. Harness your laziness and leverage it to your advantage. Store your remotes next to the TV and a book within reach of the couch.

If you are trying to write a book, when you end one session of writing, start a sentence and leave it to be finished the next day. It gives you a jumpstart and makes it easier than staring at a blank screen. It automatically overcomes inertia to get you started.

Your office/workspace matters. Fill it with useful, quality furnishings so that you enjoy being there. Remember the balance you need to maintain to keep from being distracted by your environment. Stop allowing your home office to become the place where all the things that are no longer useful in the rest of the house go to die. Invest money to create an environment that sparks and induces the level of creativity that you need to develop or create that next masterpiece or breakthrough product.

Be the master of your environment, and set yourself up for success. Design your spaces in life to inspire you. Quit thinking of dressing up your office as a luxury. Have you ever noticed how confident and full you feel when you are dressed in your best? Allow your environment to do the same.

Week 14: Change Your Environment

Reflection

1. Quick Summary

2. Key Insights

3. Personal Application

4. Meaningful Quotes

WEEK 15

Decision Fatigue

Many studies have shown that the later it gets in the day, the more the quality of people's decisions degrades. Research proves that excessive decision-making causes fatigue. This is why telemarketers want to call late in the day, and also why late-night snacking becomes so problematic.[27]

Often, a leader will fall into decision avoidance and end up settling on either the default or status-quo options. The easy and readily available options often lead to poor outcomes, or more dangerously, the *wrong* outcome.

Leaders often feel frustration prompted by people who adopt a lackey mentality and only report the news. Let's face it—if people are on your payroll, their primary function is to bring help and supply. When it comes to serving in the ministry, people often have an "I am just helping you out" mentality. Leaders in business and ministry must know and understand the fullness of what their organization does. People must see their work as important. We serve all as unto God. *As leaders, we don't need paycheck takers; we need difference makers.* There is a huge difference between making the headlines and reporting the news.

The difference between a thermostat and a thermometer is that a thermometer only reports the temperature in the room, while the thermostat controls and changes the temperature.

Sometimes our day can seem like a ceaseless train of interruptions by people who ask questions and/or need our input. We blink and the day is over, having accomplished nothing that was on our high-priority list.

My leaders and I use a system in our organizations designed to mitigate decision fatigue. We make sure every person knows that they must have three viable solutions to that problem before they bring a problem to us. This practice is very counter-intuitive, and if you try to implement this, be prepared for resistance. Immature people who just want instructions will resist this, but they must challenge themselves for your ministry or business to grow, have greater reach, and make a bigger impact.

So, we require our people to present, along with the problem, three options for solving that problem as well as their recommendation and an explanation of why they chose that particular option. Requiring three options helps you to make a decision quickly, avoiding the headache of rehashing all the details and expending unnecessary decision-making energy, and it allows you to move on to more important things more

---

[27] Tierney, John. "Do You Suffer From Decision Fatigue?" *The New York Times*, 17 Aug. 2011, www.nytimes.com/2011/08/21/magazine/do-you-suffer-from-decision-fatigue.html. Accessed 23 July 2020.

quickly. You must keep in mind that you won't accept any three options. They must be *viable solutions*, meaning they have to be *especially good choices*. Sometimes in the laziness of their thinking, people will propose the first things that come to mind. But upon further scrutiny, the options may not hold up as workable.

Here is the reality: When you only have only one option, you have no choice. The problematic situation almost dictates its answer, whether right or wrong.

Having only two options creates a dilemma. You might as well flip a coin for the answer.

Three options allow for a real DECISION. With three options, you can make a sound/informed decision.

This system accomplishes a few things:

· It forces people out of the lackey mentality, to think things through, and to do the heavy lifting of research and weighing options. According to national statistics, employers get only about 50 percent of an employee's full effort, and, in the area of thinking, even less. Unfortunately, when it comes to thinking, people tend to be inherently lazy. A prevalent problem today is that society has created many consumers and few creators and producers. Hence, one of the biggest challenges with Christianity as a whole is that people want to consume God and not commune with God. But that is a discussion for a different day.

· It ensures that employees/ministry helpers do the research and are fully versed in the problem. As they research the issue, they will often uncover more pertinent details that would contribute to a better decision. People often avoid research and just go with the first option, or the easiest route in their mind, which is to bring it to you, their leader, to solve.

· The solution isn't always one of the three options; sometimes, the three options will spur a better answer, or it may be some combination of two or three solutions.

· By requiring them to communicate which option they chose and why you have created an opportunity for training. By understanding the framework of their decisions, you are testing their understanding of your style and core values to see if they are aligned. This process offers you the opportunity to help their thinking along and allows them to grow in their independent decision-making ability. The long-term goal is to reduce the number of decisions that get brought to you and to increase their aptitude for handling things the way you want them handled.

Sometimes implementing new change can be difficult, and it takes an initial investment of time and effort, but I assure you, it will pay off in the long run.

Week 15: Decision Fatigue

Reflection

1. Quick Summary

2. Key Insights

3. Personal Application

4. Meaningful Quotes

WEEK 16

Eat More Peanuts

One day in 2007, Arianna Huffington, founder of *The Huffington Post*, was at home on the phone and checking emails when she passed out, fell, and woke up in a pool of blood with a broken cheekbone and a cut over her eye. She was reportedly working 18-hour days.[28]

At least 78 percent of American adults say their stress level increased or stayed the same over the past five years, with 33 percent saying their stress levels are affecting their mental health according to a recent report from the American Psychological Association. Almost half of adults say stress has caused bouts of insomnia within the past month, the APA report found.[29]

Alex Soojung-Kim Pang, author of *Rest: Why You Get More Done When You Work Less*, writes, "With a few notable exceptions, today's leaders treat stress and overwork as a badge of honor, brag about how little they sleep and how few vacation days they take and have their reputations as workaholics carefully tended by publicists and corporate PR firms."[30]

As a leader, whether in business or ministry, life drifts towards complexity in a manner reminiscent of the fabled "Boiling Frog." As the premise goes, if you place a frog in a pot of cold water and slowly turn up the heat, it will eventually cook because it adapts to the rising temperature. By the time it realizes that the temperature has risen too high, it is too late. However, if threw a frog into a pot of boiling water, it would hit the surface and immediately jump out.

Our lives can become much like that. If we don't pay careful attention, life's pressures gradually ratchet up until we are overwhelmed and overcooked. I call if "drift."

There is a scotoma, or blind spot, that comes from working hard *in* your business or ministry and not *on* it. A scotoma may be likened to you asking your kid to go to the kitchen and get you the cup next to the refrigerator. They already don't want to do it; they may tell you that it is not there. Upon your insistence, they get up and go look and come back with the brilliant observation that "it is not there!" You assure them

---

[28] ""Arianna Huffington: Collapse from Exhaustion Was 'Wake-up Call'." *Today.com*, NBC Universal, 2014, www.today.com/health/arianna-huffington-collapse-exhaustion-was-wake-call-2D79644042.

[29] Anderson, Norman B. American Psychological Association, 2014, pp. 3–3, *Are Teens Adopting Adults' Stress Habits?*

[30] Pang, Alex Soojung-Kim. Rest: Why You Get More Done When You Work Less. Basic Books, 2018.

that it is and send them back only for them to return once again with the statement, "It's not there." Then you have to play Captain Obvious and lead them back into the kitchen only to find that the cup is where you said it was. Of course, your retort is, "If it were a snake, it would have bit you."

We have all been through this type of scenario. It's an example of a type of scotoma. This child was not rebellious; they truly were not seeing the cup in question because of their preoccupation, disdain for the task, or simply not paying attention.

The fourth commandment is "Remember the Sabbath day, to keep it holy" (Exodus 20:8).

Biblically, in the Old Testament, no work was done on the Sabbath, and in some Orthodox religions, that prohibition is still in full effect even to this day. The traditional Sabbath is sundown on Friday to sunset on Saturday.

The idea of the Sabbath is allowing one's life to lie fallow. Sabbath keepers do not conduct work or business on the Sabbath—not even cooking. In some extreme cases, people are not allowed to flip the switch to turn on lights.

Now, don't disconnect. I am not suggesting that you give up your creature comforts. There is a principle here that I think is important. These Sabbath days should be dedicated to rest, fellowship, prayer, study, and relaxation, with no exceptions other than emergencies (sick kids and things like that).

The overarching theme is that Sabbath-keepers had to plan for the day in advance and then force themselves to rest. Think it not strange that every time people overdo it, their doctors recommend rest. In certain situations, hospitalized patients are intentionally put into a coma so they can rest.

For Old Testament Israelites, the Sabbath Day was wholly devoted to God and rest—a sort of tithe of their time, if you will. The main important part is to let the ground lie fallow.

Even in farming, the Israelites were supposed to let the ground lie fallow every seventh year. They stored up and prepared in the sixth year to rest their field in the seventh year.

That seventh year was a time for the land to recuperate and revitalize its proper nutrients. If the land goes too long without rest, the ground becomes unfruitful and cannot produce.

George Washington Carver, a.k.a. "the Peanut Man," originated and instituted a rest and rotation system for farming. By alternating soil-depleting crops like cotton with peanuts, which put essential nutrients back into the soil, he increased the overall yield of crops.[31]

You must understand that rest is essential. As New Testament believers, we understand that man was not made for the Sabbath, but that the Sabbath was made for man. Within that very statement should be our answer. If it was made for us, then we must need it. Let me be honest—why would God rest on the seventh day? Not

---

[31] "George Washington Carver." *Missouri Agriculture*, agriculture.mo.gov/gwc.php.

because He had to. God never gets tired! He did it like the "Good, Good Father" He is to demonstrate to us what we need to do.

Reflection

1. Quick Summary

2. Key Insights

3. Personal Application

4. Meaningful Quotes

WEEK 17

Open Door Policy

Having an open-door policy is the battle cry of the ineffective.

I cannot tell you how many times people have told me they have an open-door policy and gleam ear to ear with a certain level of pride.

When I hear this, I think to myself, *You have just let me know that you are inefficient, truly unproductive, and you don't value the rest of the people, employees, customers, and congregants who are counting on you.*

Before you get salty with me, let me explain.

Most people know what IQ is (Intelligence Quotient, or "book smarts"), and EQ is starting to gain traction (that is, Emotional Quotient, your ability to relate to people). AQ is Adversity Quotient, or your ability to endure, and I would like to share a new term that is much-needed in today's society. That term is FQ, "Focus Quotient"—your ability to focus. In today's fast-paced digital world, companies and service providers are hiring behavioral psychologists to hook and addict you and your children to technology and apps.

Yes! You heard that correctly—they are hiring behavioral psychologists to train them on how to create digital addictions. Many years back, Donald Trump coined a business phrase, "Cash is king!" In today's world, "Engagement is king." Mental engagement has become the new currency. Focus is becoming a precious and limited commodity. The psalmist asks God to "teach us to number our days that we may apply our hearts to wisdom" (Psalms 90:12).

Everyone competes for your focus and time. As a leader, you must be ever mindful that your productivity affects the entire organization, and if you want to be productive, you must protect what little focus you have left.

The battle for focused attention is truly the greatest fight we engage in today. Your success as the leader of a ministry or business rises and falls on your ability to do your most important work—whatever that may be! It is unique to your organization. But one thing I am sure of—if you are anything like me, you always wish you had more time. OR you spend your entire day busy and realize that you have nothing important accomplished at the end of it. So, you take a bunch of stuff home, and now your family time has been infringed on and, unfortunately, the most important people in your life suffer.

Let's say you work for a company, and you want a promotion or raise. Or you want to demonstrate your ability to rise in the ranks. The immediate clutch reaction tends to be "I need to work longer and harder to thrive."

Peter Drucker said, "There is nothing quite so useless, as doing with great efficiency, something that should not be done at all."[32]

Time is a zero-sum game, and we all have the same amount. It is the great playing-field leveler. It is the one commodity that we cannot create more of. That being said, here is the problem: Statistically, it takes 25 minutes on average to refocus after an interruption.[33] When people say they have an open-door policy, I can almost predict that they have a reduced level of effectiveness due to the constant train of people coming in and out of their office, pulling them into the trivial and mundane.

People do not expect their doctors, attorneys, or any other well-paid, respected individual, for that matter, to drop everything and come to their rescue. However, particularly in ministry and in some businesses, people expect you to be at their beck and call. But a lack of preparedness on their part doesn't constitute an emergency on my part. Even the doctor's voicemail will say, "If this is an emergency, hang up and dial 9-1-1."

As leaders, we must be careful not to compromise the bigger picture of the overall organization for the ego boost of feeling needed by dealing with the small fires—many of which are not accidents but arson. We cannot throw on a firefighter hat and run to battle every blaze when alarms go off. There are other people attached to your ministry (and employees attached to your business) who depend on you to stay at the helm and do the most vital work that moves the ball forward and makes it rain. You would be shocked at how much you can accomplish with just a few hours of uninterrupted focus time. The first time you try this, you will have to fight way harder than you should to focus for that length of time, which will show how conditioned we have become to needing constant stimuli—indoctrinated by social media.

According to an article on the top titans of the technology sector a few years back, although these people market their games, phones, and apps to children, *they do not allow their children to become addicted*. I may not agree with most of what Bill Maher says, but he made the compelling statement: "Cigarette manufacturers just wanted your lungs, and the App Store wants your soul."[34]

You cannot allow distractions to walk in when they want. Am I suggesting that you lead by abdication? Of course not! However, I would insist on scheduling everything on your calendar. That way, you can give your 100% undivided attention to what people are asking for on your terms and timetable—the same way doctors, lawyers, and other well-paid professionals do.

"But, I can multi-task!"

That's a lie! It has been proven many times over that a person cannot multi-task, only multi-switch. You can do only one thing at a time, and what you think is multi-

---

[32] 1995 October 22, The Philadelphia Inquirer, The Scene: In Bucks and Montgomery Counties by Edgar Williams, Quote Page BC3, Column 3, Philadelphia, Pennsylvania. (Newspapers_com)

[33] Mark, Gloria. The Cost of Interrupted Work: More Speed and Stress.

[34] "New Rule: Social Media is the New Nicotine | Real Time with Bill Maher (HBO) " *YouTube,* uploaded by Real Time with Bill Maher, 12 May 2017, https://youtu.be/KDqoTDM7tio

tasking is not doing more than one thing at a time, but switching between multiple priorities. You will be shocked at the amount of work you can get done when you give a project an hour or two of uninterrupted focus and stop trying to serve two masters.

In implementing this, I have noticed a few things:

· Number 1

When required to get on your schedule, people are less likely to bring nonsense to the table and tend to become more circumspect about what to bring to you.

· Number 2 People seem to get more resourceful in solving their problems. If it is easy to walk into your office and dump the problem on your desk, people will do just that.

If you have ignored all that I have just said and are still stuck on having an open-door policy, then I would submit this idea to you and take a page out of the Academic Community's Playbook:

· Designate specific times (like a college professor does) to be available so that anyone with an issue has access.

· But never forget that access is easily abused by the unskilled.

· Quit trying to get your most important work done in between distractions

· Schedule your most important task first and handle your distractions in between your most important work.

· Remember, it takes an average of 25 minutes to refocus and recover from a 3-minute question. After several of those in a day, you can begin to see why not much else gets done.

What will you do with all of the recovered time from a day of constant interruptions? I don't know. How about, go home and play with your kids? Or smooch on your husband or wife? Maybe take up a hobby or get some rest? Play some golf? But I assure you, when you treat your time as valuable, others will too.

Reflection

1. Quick Summary

2. Key Insights

3. Personal Application

4. Meaningful Quotes

WEEK 18

Productivity

Dwight D. Eisenhower was the 34th president of the United States from 1953 until 1961. Before becoming president, he served as a general in the United States Army, as the Allied Forces supreme commander during World War II, and was NATO's first supreme commander.[35]

He stated the following: "I have two kinds of problems: the urgent and the important. The urgent are not important, and the important are never urgent."

Eisenhower had to make tough decisions on the many tasks he faced each day. His frustration finally led him to invent the world-famous Eisenhower Principle, which today helps us prioritize by urgency and importance.[36]

Many leaders start their day by immediately creating a list of all the things they need to do for that day (a.k.a. the "to-do" list). Then they tend to dive right into the list by jumping into their email or morning meetings and conference calls, leaving the more complicated tasks for the afternoon.

If that sounds like your typical morning, then you're making a common mistake in managing productivity vs. optimal energy.

Besides, what if the most important task is number ten on your list, and you only get to number eight? You've wasted the entire day without touching your key priorities. Furthermore, research proves that the first few hours after waking are when your brain is at its sharpest, and you're more likely to stay on task. Why waste that time on meetings, reading emails, or returning phone calls?

Many studies conclude that people perform their best early in the day. Human psychological researchers confirm that our willpower is a finite resource. Once depleted, it's gone for the rest of the day. That is why many of our poor eating habits and choices occur later in the day (ergo, midnight snacking).

Merely having a to-do list is not enough because if you only seek to check tasks off the list, you will find that you wasted energy and focus on nonessential tasks. You should spend your early hours focusing on the highest priority items. Early morning is a great time to set aside for creating goals and strategies for the day, week, month, or even the year.

---

[35] *Dwight D. Eisenhower.* 3 Dec. 2019, www.biography.com/us-president/dwight-d-eisenhower.

[36] Oppong, Thomas. "The Eisenhower Method For Taking Action (How to Distinguish Between Urgent and Important Tasks)." *Medium*, Mission.org, 19 Jan. 2017, medium.com/the-mission/the-eisenhower-method-for-taking-action-how-to-distinguish-between-urgent-and-important-tasks-895339a13dea.

Successful leaders dedicate an average of about 25 minutes of their morning to strategizing and planning. During this time, they tackle important tasks and projects while postponing responses to emails, calls, and texts until after lunchtime.

As I mentioned earlier, Mark Twain famously said, "Eat a live frog first thing in the morning, and nothing worse will happen to you the rest of the day." There is a lesson to be learned in eating the frog first, and that is the power of directed focus.

A common productivity mistake is focusing energy on what's urgent before the important. The problem with this approach is: If you keep ignoring the important things you want to accomplish long-term, you set yourself up to be reactive when those things become both urgent and important. This is "firefighting" mode. Putting urgent things first also distracts you from acting on the most important things.

In essence, the squeaky wheel gets the grease.

Crossing seemingly urgent items off your list may feel good, but it doesn't necessarily move the needle in your personal or professional life.

I was in the office many years ago, and something happened with one of my other business units. It required my immediate attention—or, so it seemed. As I jumped up and began to explain to a colleague that I had to go, he made a comment that I have never forgotten—a life lesson that has since served me well. He said, "You are not a fireman, and you can't run around going from fire to fire."

I've had times where I felt my life was out of my control and directed by others. On a road trip a few years ago, I saw a bumper sticker that said, "Your lack of preparedness does not constitute an emergency on my part." Other people's dysfunction and challenges often lead to what seem like fires that must be put out.

This one principle will help you take back the power over your life: Others must not dictate your time.

Many people think they can manage time. That is a misnomer. Time cannot be managed, as you can never get more of it, and it waits for no man. We must learn to *maximize time* and *manage emotion as it relates to time*.

The more successful you desire to be, the more effective you have to be with your time. Warren Buffet said, "The difference between successful people and really successful people is that really successful people say 'no' to almost everything."

We must master the art of "no," so we can work on the most important priorities.

Let's start with what I call "the capture stage." The first thing to do is to take a sheet of paper and list the top three priorities that would significantly move the ball down the court for your organization (and no more than three).

Next, look through your email, text messages, notebooks, sticky notes, and wherever else you keep information and data to review all your current projects. Brain dump everything you are working on onto the back of the sheet, listing all the specific things that need to be done and their deadlines. I mean *everything*. Sometimes it helps to track a week of your activities to determine what you are currently doing as well. You can also download apps to your phone to monitor your screen time and how you're spending your time. (Only the brave have the heart to do this one.)

You will be shocked to see how much time you waste on nonessential things. Go ahead and invest the time to do that now. Before you continue reading, make a capture list.

***

Did you make your capture list? If you didn't, set this book aside and do that right now. It is a very critical step.

***

Now, let's continue.

DILEMMA Urgent / Important	**DECISION** Important / Not Urgent
DELUSION Urgent / Not Important	**DILEMMA** Urgent / Important

As you will notice on the above productivity sheet, there are four quadrants. The first quadrant is what I call *Dilemma*—this is for those things that are considered important and urgent. These are things you have to do NOW!

This area contributes to the firefighter syndrome, where you find yourself dealing with problems as they arise. These types of tasks will always hound you. Whether they were important tasks about which you procrastinated, or if they just pop up (seemingly) out of nowhere, they are now urgent.

That is why it is important to leave as much margin (or "free time") in your schedule as possible. These types of events will happen in every leader's day. There are urgent and important tasks that significantly impact your top three goals. They move the needle for your life and career and need to be done today or tomorrow at the latest.

Take a moment, go through your list, and write all of the tasks that fit into this category.

The second quadrant on the productivity sheet is what I call *Design*. These are important tasks, but they are not necessarily urgent. I place these events on the calendar and treat them as if they were a business meeting.

Are you like me in this area? I used to treat appointments with myself as flexible and subject to change. These tasks are important but not necessarily urgent yet. You should list the tasks that you need to put on your calendar in this quadrant. Dedicate the time to get out in front of these items, ensuring they are handled well before they reach the urgent stage.

Your stress will reduce dramatically when you leave fewer things unplanned and unattended. Ideally, the bulk of your time is spent in this decisive quadrant of activities.

Since you're a pro now, go ahead and fill in this quadrant with the tasks that are important and not yet urgent. Keep going; you are more than halfway there!

Okay, are you ready?

The third quadrant is *Delusion*. This is for those tasks that are urgent but not important.

For example, we have become "Pavlov-ed" (or conditioned) to respond every time the phone rings. The very annoying sound of a ringing phone or alert from a text message causes us to leap into action and respond.

You know as well as I do that most of the time, an alert or phone signal seems urgent, but in reality, it is rarely important. You could delegate responding to these messages and calls, as they are less important to you than to others, but still pretty urgent. You should keep track of delegated tasks by email, telephone, or within a meeting so you can check on their progress later. Take a moment and fill out this quadrant of activities.

The fourth and final quadrant is called *Distraction*. These tasks are not important, and they are not urgent. This includes things like mindless Internet surfing or browsing social media, watching television, or things you should not be doing at all. Often, the key to effective time management is recognizing that the things you should stop doing are as important as understanding your key priorities and objectives. These escapism-oriented tasks give you an excuse to not deal with the important tasks in the first and second quadrants.

For example, some people will spend hours cleaning their desk or office before getting their day started. It gives a false sense of accomplishment and wastes much time. I don't advocate *not* cleaning your office, but don't waste your key, emotionally strong, and best intellectual hours doing so.

To level up, pay someone to do it and keep your focus on the higher-impact and more important tasks.

If you are really bold, take everything on that list of distractions and just throw it away. (Scary, huh?)

As you can see, creating a to-do list without taking the time to determine what's important can be very hit and miss. It is not about doing things right; it is about doing the right things. This process seems tedious, and when you first get started, it will be difficult. However, if you stay with it, as you master this, your productivity and effectiveness will go through the roof!

Most people don't value planning. But if the statistic is true that one hour of preparation saves ten hours of unnecessary work, then your focus should be on spending more time on the planning process and prioritizing the correct tasks. This will give you a laser focus—and the difference between a light bulb and a laser is *the focus*.

Use your peak energy and focus on getting your highest priority tasks or hurdles out of the way, first and foremost. You will see huge results when you deal with the priorities that move the needle for your organizations.

Reflection

1. Quick Summary

2. Key Insights

3. Personal Application

4. Meaningful Quotes

WEEK 19

Ship the Product

Back in the 90s, when I worked in Information Technology, Microsoft Windows was the premier computer operating system. It went through many iterations. (I am not sure what version they are on today since I am now an Apple user.) They had a version called Windows 95. Then they released Windows 95a, then 95b, and 95c.[37]

What Microsoft did at the time was revolutionary. Most software companies beta tested their software internally and then found a select group of people to look for problems and issues with the software. When they were confident that it was ready, they ultimately shipped the product.

Microsoft changed the game when they began a type of beta testing on customers by releasing the product first, then reviewing and analyzing the problems that people reported almost in real-time. So instead of paying people to find the problems, their customers were paying to find their own problems.

If we are not careful, we can become so pedantic about our product or services being perfect that we forget to just "ship the product." You have to realize that at some point, you are buying back your results by spending so much time seeking perfection—nitpicking if you will—and not realizing that it's time to ship the product. You can become paralyzed by over-analysis and constant evaluation.

I am in no way suggesting that you put out an inferior product. However, I am suggesting that you realize there is no such thing as perfection. At some point, you must step back and ship the product. Some of the details and improvements can only come after you have released it. I have seen organizations go broke trying to perfect a product instead of releasing it to generate the capital needed to distribute version 2.0 or 3.0. (or in the case of Microsoft, 95a, 95b, and 95c.)

Beta testing allowed Microsoft to get more accurate data and make needed adjustments for actual users of their product.

You cannot become obsessed with your product or service being perfect because, in actuality, perfection doesn't exist. Sometimes you have to ship the product realizing that you cannot hold it back, trying to make it perfect. If you are not careful, your product will never make it to market, or you will start buying back your results immediately. You will reach the point of diminishing returns. Remember, when you calculate the profitability of something, you must include the time it took to produce

---

[37] "Windows 95." *Wikipedia*, Wikimedia Foundation, 19 July 2020, en.wikipedia.org/wiki/Windows_95.

the final product. Many people disregard time spent in development because there is no immediate, quantifiable, repeatable measure for it.

Let me explain. It is easy to account for expenditures of money because you see the numbers in your bank accounts, and you know if you are in the black or the red. You know whether you are in the positive or the negative. But it is not so when it comes to time, and when you invest too much of it on the inconsequential, you deplete the valuable.

That's why the Bible tells us to number our days so that we may apply our hearts to wisdom (Psalm 90:12).

You have to manage the balance of getting things ready, not perfect. Much of your growth and development will happen after you ship the product.

Start the business.

Send the letter or email.

Launch the product.

Begin it NOW!

Scottish mountaineer and writer William Hutchison Murray wrote:

Until one is committed, there is hesitancy, the chance to draw back, always ineffectiveness. Concerning all acts of initiative (and creation), there is one elementary truth, the ignorance of which kills countless ideas and splendid plans—that the moment one definitely commits oneself, then Providence moves too. All sorts of things occur to help one that would never otherwise have occurred. A whole stream of events issues from the decision, raising in one's favour all manner of unforeseen incidents and meetings and material assistance, which no man could have dreamt would have come his way. I have learned a deep respect for one of Goethe's couplets: "Whatever you can do, or dream you can, begin it. Boldness has genius, power, and magic in it!"[38]

Begin it now.

We must always know that when we come to the edge of the cliff, one of two things is certain: when we leap by faith, God will either catch us or teach us to fly.

Stop holding on to your idea, or program, or product. Sometimes you just have to ship the product!

---

[38] Murray, W. H., and Robert Anderson. *The Scottish Himalayan Expedition.* Dent & Sons, 1951.

Reflection

1. Quick Summary

2. Key Insights

3. Personal Application

4. Meaningful Quotes

WEEK 20

The Mystery of Mastery Revealed

In this section, we are going to reveal the mystery to mastery. Many people will say, "Oh, I have heard all this before."

The question isn't "Do you know it?" but "Have you *mastered* it?"

Knowing what to do and *doing what you know* are two very different things.

I have heard it said, "Set a goal so big that you can't achieve it until you grow into the person who can."

Entrepreneur Jim Rohn is quoted as saying, "You don't achieve goals; you grow into your goals." Your growth and development are two of the most important aspects of significant accomplishment.

Few people understand how mastery comes. It's a process—stages, if you will—that allow us to understand the journey of mastering any skill. If you are not careful, you can become frustrated with yourself because you don't understand that learning has a paradigm. In the movie *Blade*, Wesley Snipes's character quips, "When you understand the nature of a thing, you know what it's capable of!"[39] When you understand the process, it becomes easier to locate and facilitate your growth to the next level without becoming frustrated.

We begin our journey to mastery with *Stage One: Unconscious Incompetence*. In other words, you are unaware of what you don't know. Simply put, you don't know what you don't know; therefore, awareness must come to begin your first step into mastery.

This stage progresses into *Stage Two: Conscious Incompetence*. You become acutely aware of the lack of skill in a particular area. Because it is counter-intuitive, you have no "muscle memory," so to speak. In and of itself, this stage reveals the nature of your need to learn and change. This is the *ouch* stage because it is certainly the most laborious and tends to be fairly slow compared to the other stages. This is where learning and mistakes tend to happen. This is the place of fumbling and awkwardness as you traverse the pain of growth and development. You begin to understand new concepts and ideas. You being rewiring your understanding to accept a new paradigm, concept, or idea.

Now you progress into *Stage Three: Conscious Competence*. You are learning how to do something, but it is slow and tedious, and it requires much of your focus and frenetic energy. You have to concentrate on getting it right. Have you ever noticed that when you get lost while driving, you turn down the radio so you can concentrate

---

[39] Norrington, Stephen, director. *Blade*. New Line Cinema, 1998.

better? When you first learn how to drive, you have to think about every aspect of the basics consciously: checking mirrors, pressure on the gas pedal and brakes, staying the right distance from other vehicles, etc. But the more experienced you become as a driver, the more automatic the skillset becomes for you, a sort of robot mode, because you have mastered the routines of driving.

When I was about ten years old, I learned how to program with BASIC computer code and write games. I learned that if the computer glitched, it was not the computer, but the program that was problematic. The computer will always follow instructions. It's called "GIGO" (Garbage In, Garbage Out).

Your development in this stage requires sheer concentration. You'll often be unable to do anything else. When a person is learning a new trade or skill, they have difficulty starting a new relationship at the same time. The newness of habits and change is absorbing much of their cognitive function. Things need to settle down and take root before they can begin to do them instinctively, freeing up emotional and mental space.

John Wooden was the UCLA Bruins' head basketball coach from 1948 to 1975. Nicknamed the "Wizard of Westwood," he won ten NCAA Division 1 national championships in a 12-year period, including a record seven in a row. No other team has won more than four in a row in either men's or women's collegiate basketball.

Coach Wooden believed that learning fundamentals until they are all executed quickly, properly, and without conscious thought, is a prerequisite to playing the game. As a coach, he created drills so that all of the fundamentals were taught to the criterion that players execute them automatically.

Coach Wooden believed that drilling creates "a foundation on which individual initiative and imagination can flourish."

He had a rule that prohibited players from leaving the court until they hit ten free throws in a row. According to Wooden, he had no recollection that it made anybody late for dinner.[40]

The repetition of drills set them into robot mode, a kind of muscle memory, like a computer program that executed automatically without thinking—which, incidentally, is our *Stage Four: Unconscious Competence*. You become unaware of how competent you are. Your brain, no longer having to focus on the task, is freed to be more creative, fostering greater ingenuity. What was once unconscious incompetence has become second nature, and you now have *mastery*.

You can see the validity of the old saying that repetition is the mother of all skill. This becomes obvious, and it takes the mystery out of your development.

Paul says in 2 Corinthians 5:7 that we walk by faith and not by sight. The root of the Greek word for "walk" implies a well-beaten path that you have become so familiar with that you know how to walk it blindfolded, or without sight. Your walk of faith has become so well known that you no longer require your sight or senses to walk by it and in it.

---

[40] Sikes, John Jr. Champion Performance Coaching I: Coaching Your Team to Their Greatest Performance. Championship Performance, 2016.

You become *unconsciously competent* in your walk of faith.

It is not passion or brute force alone that will help you to become competent, but you need to understand the process of mastery that allows you to become the person who can accomplish your goals.

Reflection

1. Quick Summary

2. Key Insights

Week 20: The Mystery of Mastery Revealed

3. Personal Application

4. Meaningful Quotes

WEEK 21

Putting a Whiteboard in Your Wheelhouse

Have you ever been stumped? Ever reached a plateau or been unsure about what to do next? Have you had to make a difficult decision that left you with more questions than answers?

From time to time, I have—and continue to occasionally.

Making the wrong decision in ministry or business can prove to be fatal or, at least, very costly to the organization.

Often you can't trust everyone because, one, most people don't understand the pressures of running an organization and the weight of decision-making at this level. And two, some people don't have your best interest at heart without wanting to gain from you or exert some type of control over you.

One of the simplest yet most impactful ways that I have quickly overcome this dilemma follows.

Please forgive me for the graphic nature of this illustration, but it is the most effective analogy I can use. I am reminded of a quote from the movie *Tommy Boy*. Big Tom Callahan said there are two ways to see what a T-bone steak looks like—you can stick your head in a cow's behind or take the butcher's word for it.[41]

I choose the word of the butcher.

So here it is. I call it "putting a whiteboard in your wheelhouse."

I don't mean that you should literally go out and buy a whiteboard and install it in your office (although that is not altogether a bad idea).

I do mean that the presence of a complicated and/or difficult business or ministry decision can be daunting. By their very essence, having to make such decisions means that the problems you need to solve are outside your wheelhouse.

A wheelhouse is a place or situation in which you are advantageously at ease. It's your sweet spot, so to speak. Every tennis racket has a sweet spot, the center point that produces the greatest energy level with the least effort when you hit a ball. It is the epitome of leverage.

If the decision you need to make or the problem you need to solve were easy, you would not need to think any further about it because you would already know exactly what to do. It would be in your wheelhouse.

Many of us have tools in our wheelhouse, where the least amount of effort produces a high-performance result because of the skill level we have already

---

[41] Segal, Peter, director. *Tommy Boy*. Paramount Pictures, 1995.

obtained. In other words, some things are easy for us to do naturally and often instinctively.

Albert Einstein said, "No problem can be solved from the same level of consciousness that created it." In other words, for the best results, you will have to find someone who has "been there and done that" and gotten the proverbial T-shirt.

The whiteboard effect is working with someone else, brainstorming at the figurative shared whiteboard. This can push you deeper than if you were working alone. It has been scientifically proven that the presence of another party waiting for your next insight — be it someone physically in the same room or collaborating with you virtually — can short-circuit your natural instinct to avoid deep thinking.

It will push you into greater depths of resourcefulness and spur your best and most creative thinking, causing you to think deeply and purposely. By having someone you trust come along and work side-by-side with you on a problem, you can push each other toward deeper levels of understanding, and, therefore, toward the creation of more valuable and meaningful solutions—as opposed to going it alone.

So, "putting a whiteboard in your wheelhouse" means to add to your repertoire someone who can be of assistance and provide a whiteboard effect for creative and effective problem-solving. Simply having someone to talk through problems with, who will ask the right questions, will create a level of efficacious results that can take your business or ministry to the next level.

Decision fatigue is a real malady, and you must do something to lessen its effects. Sometimes leaving these decisions undone can cause us the greatest pain in the long term. So put a whiteboard in your wheelhouse to reenergize your decision-making capacity.

Reflection

1. Quick Summary

2. Key Insights

3. Personal Application

4. Meaningful Quotes

WEEK 22

Why Pencils Have Erasers

My mom often used the saying, "That is why pencils have erasers."

If we are not careful as leaders, our identity can become bound to our mistakes, and we will become self-deprecating—overly conscious of our shortcomings, not realizing that we have to wrestle with our natural human frailties. Character is certainly critical in the overall scheme of things, but to be successful, we must find a place of true peace even when things don't go well. The deal doesn't always close. The funding doesn't always come through. Often, as imperfect people trying to follow a perfect God in pursuit of our endeavors, we must recognize that there will be times where we will miss the mark. Whether it's our fault or not. But especially when it is our fault, we have to remind ourselves that that is why pencils have erasers.

Paul said in Philippians 3:12–14:

Not as though I had already attained, either were already perfect: but I follow after, if that I may apprehend that for which also I am apprehended of Christ Jesus.

13 Brethren, I count not myself to have apprehended: but this one thing I do, forgetting those things which are behind, and reaching forth unto those things which are before,

14 I press toward the mark for the prize of the high calling of God in Christ Jesus.

We must keep a laser-like focus on the endgame. *The enemy's trick is to get you to focus on the now and forget about the prize of your high calling and purpose.*

Proverbs 24:16 tells us that a righteous man falls seven times, but he gets back up.

You are going to make mistakes, and you will have to resign yourself to the fact that it happens to us all. Your ability to speedily recover and "get back on the horse again" is mission-critical.

Michael Jordan, the owner and chairman of the Charlotte Hornets, played 15 seasons in the NBA and is widely considered the greatest basketball player of all time. Jordan's accolades and accomplishments include ten scoring titles (both all-time records) and five MVP awards. He holds the NBA records for highest career regular-season scoring average and highest career playoff scoring average. ESPY (Excellence in Sports Performance Yearly Award) named him the greatest North American athlete of the 20th century, and he was second to Babe Ruth on the Associated Press's list of athletes of the century. Jordan is also a two-time inductee into the Basketball Hall of Fame.[42]

---

[42] Staff, NBA.com. "Legends Profile: Michael Jordan." *NBA.com*, NBA.com, 24 Aug. 2017, www.nba.com/history/legends/profiles/michael-jordan.

This incredibly gifted athlete said, "I've missed more than 9,000 shots in my career. I've lost almost 300 games. Twenty-six times, I've been trusted to take the game-winning shot and missed. I've failed over and over and over again in my life."[43]

The Bible says that if our hearts condemn us, God is greater than our hearts (1 John 3:20). We must always find ways to manage our emotions and to focus—to keep our eyes on the prize. If you keep looking back, you will certainly trip and fall. You have to stay focused on where you are going and not on where you have been.

Wayne Gretzky, arguably the greatest hockey player of all time, holds 61 National Hockey League records: 40 regular-season records, 15 playoff records, and six All-Star records. Gretzky said, "I skate to where the puck is going to be, not where it has been."[44]

We must press toward the mark. The word "press" implies that there will be resistance and that it won't be easy. But to do great things for God's kingdom, you must be willing to fail forward. That's why *pencils have erasers*. Say it with me: "Pencils have erasers."

We don't quit or give up—we get up and trust God always. Never be afraid to go back and make the correction or the adjustment. Again—because that's why, what?

You got it! Pencils have erasers.

---

[43] Blodget, Henry. "Check Out This Awesome Michael Jordan Quote About Success..." *Business Insider*, Business Insider, 3 Nov. 2011, www.businessinsider.com/michael-jordan-success-2011-11.

[44] "Wayne Gretzky." *Biography.com*, A&E Networks Television, 16 Aug. 2019, www.biography.com/athlete/wayne-gretzky.

Week 22: Why Pencils Have Erasers

Reflection

1. Quick Summary

2. Key Insights

3. Personal Application

4. Meaningful Quotes

WEEK 23

The Spirit of Mammon

One of the greatest keys to success is understanding that you never do what you do for money. As Rita Davenport says, "Money isn't everything, but it's right up there with oxygen."

In Luke 16:13, Jesus says, "No servant can serve two masters: for either he will hate the one, and love the other; or else he will hold to the one, and despise the other. Ye cannot serve God and mammon."

In the phrase "despise the other," the Greek word for "despise" means *not only to actively do something hateful, but it includes doing nothing, or indifference, or giving lesser value to*.

By way of illustration, your friends should be safe with you even when they are not around. Let me explain. Imagine you are with some people who start badmouthing your friend and you sit there and listen. Your response might tend to be, "Well, I didn't say anything bad; I just listened." That is still dishonorable. You should have corrected it or recused yourself from the conversation. People should be safe with you even when they are not present.

Many people tend to think that if they don't specifically and actively disrespect or blaspheme God, they are honoring Him. But the truth is that, in God's mind, to be *indifferent* toward the things of God and to hold the things concerning Him and His church in *lesser value* IS *to despise him*.

For example, take the story of Jacob and Esau. The Bible says that God loved Jacob and hated Esau (Romans 9:13). We know the story: Esau sold his birthright to Jacob for a bowl of stew—bean stew, at that. I hate beans, so that would have never worked for me no matter how hungry I was. I would have rather drank some water and gone to bed. (Side note: He had only been working for a day. I think he was being a little dramatic.)

However, the real lesson here is that Esau valued food more than the blessing, and Jacob loved the blessing of God so much that he did whatever it took to get it. Even from the womb. It was because Jacob put such a *priority on God* that God interpreted that as *love*, and Esau had *little value for God*, which God interpreted as *hate*. Thus, because Esau "hated" God, he reaped what he sowed.

I said all of that to say: *Don't let your motivating factor be mammon*—the spirit that rules unrighteous money

Many people say that money is the root of all evil, but in fact, it is *the love of money* that is the root of all evil. Money has no predilection whatsoever. It is a tool.

The *character of money* is *dependent upon the hands in which it sits*.

The *spirit of mammon* says to *buy and hoard*, but God says that "*to give is better than to receive.*"

The *spirit of mammon* says to *cheat* and *take advantage* wherever you can, but God says to *be honorable in business*

The *spirit of mammon* says to *take* and *steal*, but God says to *sow and reap*.

Mammon tries to offer you all that God is supposed to give you, just without God.

When people derive their security, identity, and significance from reliance on everything but God, they're under the influence of the spirit of mammon.

I believe business leaders and ministry leaders need to know *it takes money to do what we do*, but I also believe that many leaders have *conflicting views about money*. Their antagonistic view of money conflicts with their success and truly holds some back, at times even *sabotaging their potential*.

Many Christians are almost addicted to watching reality TV shows about others who have accomplished what they could have accomplished if they devoted the same amount of time to building their business or ministry, instead of watching others build theirs and trying to "keep up with the Whoevers."

Believe it or not, that is the spirit of mammon.

Some people stay in terribly abusive relationships because it's financially easier to have two incomes.

I have seen ministries receive an offering for a guest speaker, and they gave the speaker less and pocketed the difference because more came in than they expected. That's the *spirit of mammon*.

Some people get a job transfer, and they up and leave their church because the offer was too good to pass up on. And they think it was God's leading because the job pays a higher dollar amount.

Characteristics of the Spirit of Mammon
- Mammon is always narcissistically oriented.
- The spirit of mammon will lead you to a different doctrine.
- Mammon will try to convince you that money is equal to spirituality, which is certainly not true. If it were, pimps and drug dealers would be the most spiritual people on the planet.
- Inability to Sabbath. I take a day of rest every Monday. After sitting with my congregation all day Sunday, every Monday is my complete day off. (See how much you difference-makers mean to me?) I have a 24-hour period of rest and detachment from the pull of ministry and business to let the ground lie fallow. It is my way of letting Satan know that I will rest in the Lord, my God, and trust that things will get handled without me. I will do a resource on that later.

When you take ownership of the fact that God is truly in control and your reliance is on Him, then and only can you realize that money is a tool for the purposes, plans, and pursuits of the Master.

In Luke 16, Jesus says that money is the least of all things. If you can't manage unrighteous money, how will you be trusted with the true riches? How we manage our relationship with money is very important to God. We must value the Giver more than the gift. And as Ecclesiastes says, "Money answers all things." We need it to be available and be vessels for God to direct and use as He sees fit as a blessing to the kingdom's work. I think you are starting to see that if Satan can pervert your view of money, he can keep it out of God's hood where it can do the most good.

· Money becomes unfruitful for the kingdom when it is yielded to mammon.

· We don't do what we do for money; we do it for a purpose.

First John tells us that for this purpose, the Son of God was manifested, that He might destroy the works of the devil. Jesus was here for a purpose, and we must understand that our purpose is to affect Jesus' purpose.

We must be careful to know that the love of money isn't just the pursuit of money but the pursuit of money for the wrong purpose and allowing money, instead of the Holy Ghost's leading, to guide our decisions.

· Stingy people have the same problem as greedy people.

Remember that building a successful brand is not about being famous; it's about being exceptional. There's a big difference between famous and infamous. Both tend to be remembered—but for drastically different reasons.

Choose to do what you do to make a difference and an impact for the body of Christ, never allowing either abundance or lack to drive the ship. And the money will always come.

Reflection

1. Quick Summary

2. Key Insights

3. Personal Application

4. Meaningful Quotes

WEEK 24

The First Three Letters in "Diet" are D-I-E

Every year in January, gym memberships swell with people who have decided to get healthy. Usually, by February, the crowds subside, and many have forgotten their health goals. I have been working toward my own health goals and have made some progress. I am in no way an expert and have not yet arrived, but since my highest weight, I have lost around 80 pounds with about 50 to 60 more to go.

I've created a few tips that I think are important for anyone who wants to improve their health. While I have not perfected this by any means, I have learned a few things on my way to the scale. I am not a doctor, so check with your physician before making any drastic lifestyle changes. (I've inserted that disclaimer for the lawyers.)

I don't do diets because the first three letters of the word diet are D-I-E. The first thing you have to understand is that food is critical to your health. But fad diets often do more harm than good.

"Let food be thy medicine, and let medicine be thy food." This famous quote is often attributed to Hippocrates. While its origin may be subject to some debate, I believe it to be a truth. In Daniel 1:8, Daniel requests that he and his three friends would not have to eat the rich, unhealthy food that the Babylonian king requires his men to eat. Daniel offers a sort of wager, saying if he could eat water and veggies for ten days, the official could compare his health with that of the king's men who eat the choicest of foods and see how they fare. Daniel 1:15 says, "At the end of the ten days, Daniel and his three friends looked healthier and better nourished than the young men who had been eating the food assigned by the king."

Healthy eating requires lifestyle changes and choices that become more than a diet; they are a way of life. Here are six points that I believe will be very helpful.

1. Drink more water. When you first wake up, drink at least 8–12 ounces of water immediately. Get your day started with more water. The more water you drink, the fuller you feel, and the less you will eat. You will be surprised at how your body retains water, and when you start to drink more, it will begin to release water and help jumpstart your weight loss journey by shedding unnecessary water weight.

2. Reorganize. Take the time to reorganize your kitchen and refrigerator. Make all of the healthy things in your cabinets easily accessible, and make everything that is not so healthy hard to reach. Often our eating and snacking are mindless, and we gravitate toward what is easy to grab. Make healthier choices easier to find. Super pro tip: If you want to go hard in the paint, throw out all of the unhealthy things and don't have them in the house in the first place. Now you can avoid them as opposed to trying to resist them. But do it now before you change your mind. Remove all other

foods and snacks from your countertops except a bowl of fruit. Make a point to get rid of the not-so-subtle cues that are around you every day. And empty the containers directly into the garbage lest you be tempted to pull those Cheetos back out later.

Believe me, you are not getting up in the middle of the night and driving to the store to get you a snack.

3. Use a smaller plate. Plate sizes have drastically increased over the years. So be purposeful to use small plates. Use your natural tendencies toward laziness to help you with portion control. You will not want to keep getting up over and over again.

4. Serve food restaurant-style and not buffet style. Don't bring the whole dish and place it on the table. Create plates like restaurants do, and serve them that way. This strategy allows for immediate portion control and helps with mindless eating. Also, portion out snacks as opposed to grabbing the whole bag or box. Divide up portions according to the package labeling when you get home from the grocery store. You will be shocked at what the label considers a serving.

5. READ ALL LABELS. I repeat! Read the label! Know the math of units of measurement (calories, grams, ounces) and understand the ingredients. In my opinion, the obesity, diabetes, and heart-disease health crises we're facing are rooted in how much fat, salt, and sugar manufacturers add to make low-quality food taste better. Read the labels. Know the recommended portion sizes and understand the ingredients in the processed foods you eat.

6. Prepare and eat food that is closest to its natural form. Avoid anything that comes in a box or a can. Try to avoid highly processed foods. While they may be convenient, they are truly the culprit stealing our health. In other words, get the fresh green beans instead of the canned ones. Be careful not to overcook your vegetables, as cooking tends to deplete its nutritive value. The nutritive value of fresh foods is so much higher, and you will require less of it to be full. Food that is good for you doesn't have to taste bad. Experiment with flavors and options. Try new things. There are plenty of keto and even vegan alternatives that can replace unhealthier meal choices. Better food starts with better ingredients.

Let's recap. You will need to
1. drink more water,
2. reorganize,
3. use smaller plates,
4. serve food restaurant-style and not buffet style,
5. read all labels, and, finally,
6. prepare and eat foods that are closest to their natural form.

Please be mindful that you need your body to finish your race. Many people spend their health trying to get wealth and then their wealth trying to get health. Now is the time to snatch back the power of you.

Week 24: The First Three Letters in "Diet" are D-I-E

Reflection

1. Quick Summary

2. Key Insights

3. Personal Application

4. Meaningful Quotes

WEEK 25

The $6-Million Mistake

Birds of a feather flock together. Renowned businessman Jim Rohn said, "You are the average of the five people you spend the most time with."[45] Do you know what that means? Everyone in your life matters.

Some people say, "Surround yourself with positive people and eliminate the toxic ones." But it just isn't that simple. We can clearly see the polarity between those two groups of people. But we often miss the effect that the ones we deem as neutral can have on our lives.

We consider them harmless because they have been around for a while or have been a help to us at one time. There are a myriad reasons why we maintain some of the associations that we do.

If you have been a believer for any amount of time, you know that Satan never reveals himself with horns and a pitchfork. Instead, he comes very subtly disguised. "Neutral" people (those we deem neither good nor bad) are just as much of a problem as those who are negative.

Success is a zero-sum game, which means nothing is neutral—it is either for us or against us, with no in-between. While there is a certain validity to ridding ourselves of overtly toxic people, sometimes the pruning we need to do is not so obvious.

The biblical story of Hanun from 2 Samuel chapter 10 describes how Hanun ascended to the throne of the Ammonites upon the death of his father, Nahash, the former king.

King David sent his ambassadors to convey his condolences and support, remarking that Hanun's father had shown him kindness and wanted to do the same in return. But upon the counsel of his closest advisors, Hanun humiliated the emissaries, stripping them of their clothes and shaving off half of their beards.

Ultimately Hanun allied with the Syrian king against David, but he was eventually defeated and deposed. His brother, Shobi, was made king in his stead and became a loyal vassal of David's.

In Luke 6:39, the Bible posits the question: "Can the blind lead the blind?" Many answer no. But that is not true, because the Word tells us the blind can lead the blind if they're both willing to fall into a ditch.

---

[45] Groth, Aimee. "You're The Average Of The Five People You Spend The Most Time With." *Business Insider*, Business Insider, 24 July 2012, www.businessinsider.com/jim-rohn-youre-the-average-of-the-five-people-you-spend-the-most-time-with-2012-7.

Hanun had surrounded himself with people who convinced him that David had ill intent. If he had the right people who were really for him, they would have viewed David's actions in light of his intentions. When people don't understand honor, they don't know when honor is shown. More importantly, they don't know when honor is violated. Hanun's father, Nahash, was undoubtedly honorable. Most likely, he raised Hanun to understand honor. Hanun should have known what honor looked like from observing his father.

However, having the wrong people around him skewed his view and caused him to create an enemy of his own making.

When David heard about this shameful act of disrespect and how his emissaries were mistreated, he told his group to stay away until their beards grew back so they could avoid the shame of returning home and being seen in a dishonorable light.

That's true honor. According to one historical estimate, it cost Hanun 38 tons of silver (approximately 6 million dollars in today's money) to raise and equip an army to defend himself against King David, who initially was trying to honor and support him. David could have been Hanun's formidable ally like he was for his father and eventually became for his brother, who succeeded him on the throne.

All this expense and loss of life came upon Hanun because he accepted bad counsel from the wrong people—people who had no understanding of honor. He surrounded himself with people who saw King David's actions in light of their character, and it cost Hanun everything.

When referring to that "one friend," I have heard people say, "Oh, that's just So and so, you know how they are." And they will explain away bad character because it hasn't affected them in a directly visible way … yet.

Often people will say, "I don't want to judge." Don't get me started down that rabbit trail.

As leaders, we must carefully select those closest to us and guard the holding of that position in our lives as a privilege for them. If you know someone's character stinks, put some distance between you and them—you will be glad you did.

As you read this, most likely, the name of an individual or individuals come to mind. Don't ignore that prompting. It may be time for you to have some difficult conversations.

Week 25: The $6 Million Mistake

Reflection

1. Quick Summary

2. Key Insights

3. Personal Application

4. Meaningful Quotes

WEEK 26

Develop Your Team into Elite Players

I'm frequently asked, "How do you develop your team into elite players?" The simple answer is, "You don't!"

All right, well, that's our time for today. Thanks for reading.

Just kidding. Allow me to explain.

People will say things like, "How do you create employee buy-in?" Or, "People in my ministry don't care." Or, "My team is just looking for a paycheck."

Let me ask you this: When a professional football team wants to find new players, do they start a farm that grows great football players? No! They scout and recruit. They find the best talent they can find and can afford.

I think there is an overall perception that when Jesus found his disciples, they were all poor and unskilled. But, I assure you that with proper study of the Word, you will come to find that while these men may not have been as spiritual as they needed to be, they were successful in some capacity. In most cases, they were people of affluence and influence. If you have nothing to walk away from to follow Christ, then there can't be much of a sacrifice in following Him.

This is a great lead-in to the main point—you don't create elite players; you recruit them. You hire them. They may still need to have edges knocked off of them, to take them from good to great, but I assure you, no amount of development will take a poor team player and make them into a "beast." They have to do that for themselves.

The only person you can develop is yourself. You have to become skilled at recognizing great talent and ability in people and then creating systems to draw those things out of them. Sometimes people on our team are in the right church, but they are sitting in the wrong pew.

Talented people will figure out *how*, when you give them a compelling enough *why*. When you spend the time on the front end hiring the right people, it saves you stress, time, energy, and money on the back end. According to an estimate done by Recruiting.com, a bad hire can cost almost 240 thousand dollars.[46]

Wow!

When you factor in on-boarding, training, disruption to the business, their salary wasted, initial hiring cost, and last, but certainly not least, mistakes, failures, and lost opportunities for potential business because they missed it or the demand for

---

[46] Veylan, Bhavani. "Successful Hiring Starts at Your Career Site." *Corporate Career Sites and Recruiting Software - Recruiting.com*, www.recruiting.com/.

unnecessary supervision caused you to miss out—you can see how the numbers add up.

While I believe there isn't an exact formula for hiring people, I think there are some fundamentals that will work for you if you put a SYSTEM in place. Notice how I snuck in my definition of SYSTEM earlier—it is Saves You Stress, Time, Energy, and Money. If you put a system in place, you will find that it helps to weed out the riff-raff.

Let's take a look under the hood of our organization.

When we hire someone onto our executive team, we use a multi-step process. It is extensive, but it totally weeds out the wrong people quickly.

- Step One is a *clear, high-quality ad*. Make sure you have thought through what you want this to say to attract the right applicants.
- Step Two is an *online questionnaire*.
- Step Three is *submission of resumé, short online video, personality assessment, references*.
- Step Four is an *initial interview*.
- Step Five is a *second interview*.
- Step Six is a *third interview with team members, Shark Tank* style.
- Step Seven is an *interview with me* directly.
- Step Eight is to confirm references.

Reflection

1. Quick Summary

2. Key Insights

3. Personal Application

4. Meaningful Quotes

WEEK 27

Develop Your Team into Elite Players - Part 2

In recent months, we ran an ad for a position for which we received no less than 500 initial inquiries. Those initial inquiries were directed to an online questionnaire, which maybe 150 people filled out. That reduction in numbers saved us from reviewing 350 résumés of people who were not committed or interested enough to take that minimal first step. Sometimes people are just spamming their résumés out into the ethos and are very noncommittal. We got rid of those right off the bat.

The questionnaire then asks them (1) to create a short video and upload it to a media site to share it with us, (2) to email their résumé and references, and (3) to take then share with us the results of a free online personality assessment (for which we include a link).

The reason for the video is not to assess vanity, although how they dress and present themselves must match the professionalism of the company. You would be shocked at some of the videos we have received. But the most important part is to see if they have the technical skill and ability to record a video and the gumption to put it online for us to see. We need skilled and confident people, and this process weeds out those who are not tech-savvy or confident.

See, we created a SYSTEM to do the work of weeding them out for us.

The personality assessment is free. If they take it, that's great, but we also give them the option of providing an assessment if they have one already. If they choose the free route, that is fine. But we give them "extra credit," if you will, when they send us one they have paid for. It demonstrates that they are serious about their development. We are watching them like a football scout analyzing potential players to see how they handle our requests. Can they follow the instructions thoroughly?

I think you can see the pattern. This entire part of the process is accomplished with no extra work time or money invested on our end.

When we reached this point with our recent search, we had received about 25 fully completed submissions, and we ultimately did a first interview with ten or so of them.

Can you see that out of five hundred potential applicants, we created a funnel that weeded out over 90 percent of the fluff? I explain this process in more detail in our one-day intensive LeaderSHIFT Success Masterclass.

At this point, we begin interviewing the applicants, which involves a series of multiple interviews with different people. Here is an advanced tip: *Always have someone other than you conduct the initial three interviews.* Ask a mentor, a close friend, a trusted advisor, another employee, a spouse to provide an outside assessment. Sometimes we can become so desperate to fill a position, and we will kiss way too many frogs and come up with warts.

The final interview should always be with you. If the process is handled correctly, very few applicants will make it to that stage.

Reflection

1. Quick Summary

2. Key Insights

3. Personal Application

4. Meaningful Quotes

WEEK 28

The Four C's of Recruiting

Ken Fisher, the founder and executive chairman of Fisher Investments, started his company with only $250. His company now has about $100 billion in assets under management, and he is personally worth approximately $4 billion. When asked about his success and growing his company, Fisher said (and I am paraphrasing) that he quit his way to the top.[47]

Peter Drucker said, "Efficiency is doing things right; effectiveness is doing the right things." If you have been in business or ministry for longer than ten minutes, you know there is never a shortage of things to do. Leaders in today's world should not aspire to be like the Maytag man sitting around, waiting for the phone to ring to have something to do. Leaders have so much going on that they need to master the art of following Ken Fisher's example of "quitting their way to the top." Recruiting the right people to help is mission-critical for any leader's success. I am talking about *difference makers* and not just *paycheck takers*.

If you are dealing with a volunteer staff, you may be tempted to think that the same rules don't apply. But I assure you they do. Building a team of the right people is one of the most important functions you as a leader can do.

Proverbs 26:10 (AMP) says, "Like a [careless] archer who [shoots arrows wildly and] wounds everyone, so is he who hires a fool or those who [by chance just] pass by."

We will sometimes be tempted to hire to pain and not to plan. Having a thriving business or ministry can often create pain. As leaders, we are uniquely gifted at "getting rid of the pain." Our minds can become consumed with the idea of trying to eliminate pain, usually at the expense of the long-view plan. In trying to eliminate a certain pain quickly, we place people in positions under the premise that somebody is better than nobody. While it may relieve the pain's immediate sharpness, this line of thinking creates a longer-lasting pain that tends not to end well. We must slow down and think things through and be strategic about placing people in positions as we recruit to plan and not to pain.

If you want to leverage and scale your ministry or business, you will need to start quitting many of your current tasks and functions. Some of your functions have a very low return. Yes, I know that often in your mind, it is easier to just "do it yourself." But it is a form of narcissism to think you are the only one who knows how

---

[47] "Kenneth Fisher." *Wikipedia*, Wikimedia Foundation, 1 June 2020, en.wikipedia.org/wiki/Kenneth_Fisher.

to do things correctly. Remember, it is *not about doing things right*; it is about *doing the right things*.

And more importantly, your highest and best use is what you must be focused on. So, you're going to have to become a quitter! You're going to have to quit just about everything until you are doing only the key functions that *only you can and should do*. There are people who love to do the things that you hate to do. Therefore, it is better to recruit someone who can handle some of those tasks, so you can offload them and free yourself to keep the main thing *the main thing*.

This is not just for business owners or ministry heads, but also for those who may work in a particular department. Over the years, I have held positions in companies where I started out at the bottom and worked my way up to the C-level. I quickly learned that I could never be promoted if I am the only one who knows how to do the job. It takes an immense amount of security to know that you cannot derive your sense of self-worth from being the one who knows it all. You will handicap your organization and quickly become the bottleneck. You can structure your organization for growth, or you can structure it for control. But never both!

Regardless of where you are in your company or organization, I want to share with you a framework for recruiting. Please understand that recruiting carries with it the idea of specifically looking for and finding the "right" person—not just any person. Recruiting is strategic in its intent, and having a clear and proven framework helps to produce above-average results.

Statistics tell us that the average employee gives only about 50 percent of their effort to the job, and one great hire can handle three average people's workload. I think it's worth learning how to get it right.

So, the first C in the 4C framework is *Capacity*. Does this person possess the skillset to accomplish and the aptitude to understand the requirements of the position?

This is where skills and abilities must be evaluated correctly to determine someone's strengths and weaknesses. These can be very difficult to assess initially because oftentimes when you are interviewing or watching people for promotion, you are not dealing directly with them; you are dealing with their representative.

Let me explain: People are often campaigning—what I call "shaking hands and kissing babies like a politician on the stump." Not until pressure is applied do you begin to see who they really are and to discern their true skillset relating to actual performance rather than mere potential. As a pastor, I have to be extra careful because I often see people in light of their potential and not through the lens of their actual performance.

Don't fall into the trap of thinking that skill is not important. Although God used David to calm King Saul's troubled soul by lightly playing the harp, David was already a skilled musician. God added his "super" upon David's "natural." We often see people in light of how God sees them, so we speak to their potential, but we must watch for their performance.

You may have hired or promoted people at some time, and they have made a mess of things. Your first thought might tend to be that you missed God. The truth is that sometimes God was giving that other person the opportunity of a lifetime and they missed it. With God, all things are possible, but with man, everything is a risk.

Reflection

1. Quick Summary

2. Key Insights

3. Personal Application

4. Meaningful Quotes

WEEK 29

The Four C's of Recruiting - Part 2

In part 1, we discussed the importance of hiring to plan and not to pain. While it may seem like it eases the pain to place just anyone quickly into a position, I assure you it always has far-reaching repercussions that, in the long term, cause more damage than good. You don't want to roll the proverbial dice with the ministry or business that God has entrusted you with. What you do is a huge responsibility—one that you must handle with intentionality.

The Bible says to lay hands on no man suddenly (1 Timothy 5:22). That doesn't mean, "Don't slap anyone quickly." It means don't be too quick to put someone in a position without the proper vetting—as we have been discussing in the 4C recruiting framework. Our first C was Capacity—Does the person possess the skillset to accomplish and the aptitude to understand the requirements of the position?

The second C is *Commitment*. This one is a little harder to assess if you haven't had the privilege of working with the person already. But if you create an elaborate interview process such as I've described, you will be able to see their ability to "stick it out" so to speak. When most applicants are spamming their résumés out into the ethos, trying to expend as little energy as possible, you need to be careful that your process has built-in steps to vet a person properly. You want to keep them from assuming that it is easy to waste your time. Successful leaders need to be slow to hire and quick to fire.

If you have the privilege of being able to observe a person—maybe you serve together, or maybe they work in a different part of the organization—and you are considering them for a promotion, here are some ways to gauge their commitment.

- Do they show up on time and consistently?
- Are they stepping up to help, or do they watch the clock?
- Are they constantly keeping track of effort, time, and energy?
- If they serve in ministry, do they tithe?
- Are they quick to support events and functions?

These are all indications of their commitment level. You have to understand that a person's commitment level is not in their title; it is in the person. You might think if you give them the position, they will step up to meet the demand. While that can happen in limited situations, trust me when I tell you—it rarely does. You want to see if they are qualified for the position before you give them the title. Biblically, people were not given the title prior to the anointing. The anointing was on them, and the title confirmed what God was doing in them.

The third C is *Chemistry*. Chemistry is often sacrificed at the expense of the "don't judge" crowd. If a cat is being rubbed the wrong way, you have two options: either turn the cat around or switch the direction of the rub. We believers have the spirit of God on the inside of us, and we have to be careful because sometimes people will rub us the wrong way, and it is actually the Spirit of God leading us to keep them at a distance. It doesn't mean we can't love, respect, and value them. It just means they can't be too close to us because it causes a rub or agitation.

Here are a couple of questions you need to know about your chemistry with another person:
- Do they Get along with you?
- Are they *compatible* with the organization and the leadership?
- Is there *synergy*? Synergy is where two plus two equals more than four. Synergy is where the outcome is greater than the sum of its parts.
- Does this person jell with others in the company or ministry? I don't care how skilled they are if they don't fit or don't get along well with others in the organization.

Culture is affected by the people in it. By adding the wrong person to your team, your organization's culture can turn toxic fast if you're not careful. One bad apple does, in fact, spoil the bunch. You have to guard your team like you would guard your family or home. You don't let everyone or everything into it, no matter how capable they may appear to be. If they can't harmoniously bring their gift and not upset the apple cart, you are better off passing on them and waiting for the right person. They might have your hands, but if they don't have your heart, there will inevitably be a problem. For most leaders, waiting is hard; but your patience here will pay off.

Reflection

1. Quick Summary

2. Key Insights

3. Personal Application

4. Meaningful Quotes

WEEK 30

The Four C's of Recruiting - Part 3

Let's review:
We have discussed the importance of hiring to plan and not to pain.
We cannot place just anyone quickly into a position.
We don't want to roll the proverbial dice with the ministry or business God has entrusted to us.

Regarding the 4C recruiting framework, our first C is Capacity—Do they possess the skillset to accomplish and aptitude to understand the requirements of the position?

Our second C is Commitment—Are they willing to go through a hiring process, or are they just spamming out résumés looking for low-hanging fruit? If you have the privilege of serving or working together in some capacity, you have an advantage. Do they show up on time and consistently? Are they stepping up to help, or do they watch the clock? Are they constantly keeping track of effort, time, and energy?

The third C is Chemistry—Is there a rub or an agitation? Do they get along with you? Are they compatible with the organization and the leadership? Is there synergy? Does this person jell with others in the company? The culture of your organization can turn toxic quickly if you're not careful.

The fourth C in our 4C recruiting framework is *Character*. Remember, most people are *hired for capacity* and *fired for character*. In other words, they are *hired for potential* and *fired for performance*. Here are some character questions:

- Are they trustworthy, honest, forthcoming, and transparent?
- Do they display godly character?
- Are they teachable?
- Do they make adjustments quickly and adapt and learn as needed?

If you are observing and listening to them carefully, you will begin to see the fruit of who they are.

Character comes from two words: char, meaning "to burn" and actor, meaning "to act." People will *act* according to *what has been burned into* them. We must be acutely aware of the fact that pressure does not build character—it reveals it. Time will reveal who they are. So remember to hire slowly and fire quickly. As you evaluate people, your goal is not to fill someone else's cup but to empty yours. You must understand that you have to deposit what you know into others so that they can help you.

Do you know where the most expensive real estate in the world is? In New York City, real estate prices are almost $1,800 per square foot. San Francisco's real estate goes for $900 per square foot. Putting it in context, building a house costs about $75–

$100 per square foot. However, the world's most expensive real estate is the cemetery—where all dreams, visions, great ideas, and knowledge go to die.

Paul told Timothy in his second letter to him, the book of 2 Timothy, to entrust all that he had learned to capable, faithful, and trustworthy men who were able to teach others. You have much knowledge, skill, and so on inside you, and if you want to scale your organization, you need help.

Moses had Aaron and Hur to help hold up his arms (Exodus 17:12), and you, likewise, need faithful people who will help carry your organization's vision—not just your hands, but your heart as well.

Here is a little bonus: Now that you have recruited your help, what do you do? Quit!

Seriously, say it with me—QUIT! I am not advising you to delegate tasks by abdication. Meaning no birth by fire.

Jesus taught a very clear pattern for training. He took all of his disciples and invited them to follow and watch him do His ministry. Then He allowed them to do ministry together. Finally, He sent them out two-by-two to do what He had taught them to do and report back how it went.

When developing your new recruits, you want to go from (1) hands on to (2) hands in to eventually (3) hands off. First, you need to script it, meaning, write down precisely *what* you want, *how*, and *why* so your expectations are clear.

While this is formula may seem very simple, it is highly insightful and practical. Follow these simple steps:

1. Have them watch/shadow you as you do it.
2. Do it together with them. This is the place for them to ask all their questions.
3. You watch them do it. *Do not allow them to move on* to step 4 until they can completely execute the requirements of their tasks without your involvement. If there are still questions or concerns, you move back to step 2 (doing it together) until they can execute completely on their own—and I mean completely. Then, lastly, you move on to—
4. Let it go.

If you have to micromanage, you have two issues at hand. Either you have not trained them correctly or are the wrong person. Start with *retraining* as that most likely is the issue if you have spent the time on the front end, making sure you have an elite player. If not, then it is time to either *find them a different seat on the bus* or *liberate them out into the market place and start over*. Team members can be on the same bus as you want to go in the same direction as you, but they may be in the wrong seat. To put it a different way, they are in the right church just in the wrong pew.

Here's a quick recap of the 4C's of recruiting framework to remind you what qualities you are looking for:

- Capacity: Do they have the skills?
- Commitment: Are they willing to stick it out and be invested?
- Chemistry: Do they get along and fit?

- Character: Can you trust them? Are they honest and forthright?

And finally, remember people tend to hire for capacity and fire for character. Just being talented doesn't make someone a good fit.

Reflection

1. Quick Summary

2. Key Insights

3. Personal Application

4. Meaningful Quotes

WEEK 31

Getting Outside Help Training

Jim Collins, author of *Good to Great*, said the following: "Leaders of companies that go from good to great start not with 'where' but with 'who.'" They start by getting the right people on the bus, the wrong people off the bus, and the right people in the right seats. And they stick with that discipline—first the people, then the direction—no matter how dire the circumstances.

Most leaders focus on herding everyone onto the same bus so they can all go in the same direction. However, they tend to forget about making sure the right people are in the right seats on the bus. Organizational balance and alignment are key. They're like the difference between music and noise.

Many people think if sound is too loud, then it's noise. But if that's true, how do you explain rock concerts? Some feel that this difference is based on the music's intended purpose, but how do we explain smooth jazz meant to calm and praise and worship meant to glorify or setting the alphabet to a song so that our kids can learn? In actuality, the difference between noise and music lies in order and structure.

As a leader, your job is like that of a choir director or bandleader, bringing order and structure from all the individual parts to create a harmonious symphonic sound.

Just providing a bus is not enough. Neither is just knowing where the bus is going. Even having the right people on the bus is not enough on its own. I think you get the idea.

You must have the right people on the right bus in the right seats going in the right direction while leaving behind the wrong people.

And once all of that training is in place, you need *the next important key*. Having *skilled workers* is more important than you think. A certain amount of training can be accomplished in-house—onboarding if you will—but I am talking about the continual development of your staff and teams.

Most of us tend to fare better when we use outside help. Whether in a church, ministry, or business, people tend to become familiar with their leaders, so training and developing employees and staff members become increasingly difficult. They lose the ability to "hear" your voice. Even Jesus could do no mighty works in His hometown because of their familiarity with Him before starting His public ministry. He actually remarked in Mark 6:4 that a prophet is honored everywhere else, but not in his home town and among his own people.

In this situation, you have to find a trusted voice with a proven system that people are not familiar with outside your organization. That's why the body of Christ has as many parts to it as there are to the natural body.

Many leaders see training as an unnecessary expense, but I tell you, it is SOOOO important. I invest 10 percent of my income on my training and development. And I take it one step further than just what I make—I actually invest 10 percent of what I *want* to make.

On average, the return on training is around 33%.[48] That means if I hand you a dollar, you give me back a $1.33 for my return on investment (ROI). For example, if I want to make 250K annually, then rather than spend, I invest 25K annually on my development and growth. I will attend mentor's meetings and take advantage of their services and resource materials— books, CDs, conferences, podcasts, and online training.

Benjamin Franklin is quoted as saying, "An investment in knowledge always pays the best interest."[49]

Businesses in the U.S. spent more than $70 billion on employee training initiatives alone.[50]

Why would they do that? They recognize the ROI.

When you can guarantee a return, it's like manufacturing money. Many companies are reluctant to invest in training and development, especially during an economic downturn. But that is the wrong move.

According to the Association for Talent Development, companies that offer comprehensive training have 218% higher income per employee than companies without formalized training. These organizations also enjoy a 24% higher profit margin than those who spend less on training.[51]

In a study conducted by the National Center on the Educational Quality of the Workforce, increases in education were three times more effective at increasing productivity than spending money on better equipment.

One research project commissioned by a university said 74% of employees felt that they weren't achieving their full potential at work due to lack of training.[52]

Outside training overcomes the problems associated with the familiarity of in-house voices, and it begins to establish a baseline:

- To standardize the framework of thinking.

---

[48] Nasta, Sanjay. "Training ROI: Using Return on Investment for Training Programs." *Microassist*, 21 July 2018, www.microassist.com/learning-dispatch/training-roi/.

[49] Franklin, Benjamin. Franklin's Way to Wealth, or, "Poor Richard Improved.". Printed and Sold by S. Wood, 1982.

[50] Bersin, Josh. "Spending on Corporate Training Soars: Employee Capabilities Now A Priority." *Forbes*, 4 Feb. 2014, www.forbes.com/sites/joshbersin/2014/02/04/the-recovery-arrives-corporate-training-spend-skyrockets/#3a72e76dc5a7.

[51] "Profiting from Training!: Rewards from Management Training." *Business Training Experts*, 9 June 2016, businesstrainingexperts.com/knowledge-center/training-roi/profiting-from-learning/.

[52] [52] Gutierrez, Karla. *Mind-Blowing Statistics That Prove the Value of Employee Training and Development*, 2017, www.shiftelearning.com/blog/statistics-value-of-employee-training-and-development.

- It turns noise into music by giving everyone similar skills and knowledge.
- It standardizes the language and vernacular they use.
- It creates consistent organization-wide understanding so that synergy can occur.

What exactly is synergy, and why is it so important? Synergy is 2+2=>4. The "whole" you end up with as people interact and share their energy and ingenuity is greater than the sum of its parts. Alignment produces efficiency and speed. To get the most benefit from outside training, the first thing you need to do is find training that will solidify the skills required for your specific organization. There is a difference between "just in time" knowledge and "just in case" knowledge. Investing money in just in time is always better than just in case. Some knowledge you need for now, and some things you should have just in case. If you don't already have some type of training available or a company already in mind, we would love for you to consider our LeaderSHIFT Success Masterclass. It will help get you and your team to the next level, and it's guaranteed. God has given us the vision to equip, inspire, and influence extraordinary people, leaders, and organizations to impact the world for His glory. We are available to conduct private workshops and training on location with your organization. Please visit our website m4.geneherndon.com/lsm or join our Facebook Group, #LEVELUP, for details on upcoming events and more resources.

We stand at the ready to help in whatever way we can.

Reflection

1. Quick Summary

2. Key Insights

3. Personal Application

4. Meaningful Quotes

WEEK 32

If You Don't Have One, You Are One

By the time most leaders know that they need to hire someone, they are already stewing in the pressure cooker. Like that proverbial boiling frog, they have adjusted to the gradually rising heat of their work environment. If we are not careful as entrepreneurs, we will find ourselves in the midst of the chaos of doing our business or ministry, having adjusted to it so gradually that by the time we recognize the problem, we're half-cooked and can't climb out of the pot.

There are two major expenses that entrepreneurs have to be monitor. No matter the size of your company—whether large, small, or midsized—this is a universal truth across all business sizes and industries.

These two expenses are (1) brick and mortar, that is, buildings, and (2) human capital. Simply stated: buildings and people. If you notice, whenever you hear of a company not performing well, they are either laying off (people) or shutting down locations (brick and mortar.)

The time to understand and evaluate your initial hiring decisions is from the very outset of your business. Years ago, I was in real estate. I was in the top percentile in the Southwest region for a large national franchise, of which I ultimately became a part-owner. Early in my career, I was in the office, and one of the other agents asked me how I did so well in real estate. I explained to her that the first thing I did when I entered the business was to build a team, starting with my assistant. She then replied, "You have an assistant?"—with a level of shock, disdain, and slight envy.

I quipped back, "If you don't have one, you are one," and walked away. I was quick with the wit and a little less saved back then.

As business and ministry leaders, we must understand early on the importance of decisions regarding "brick and mortar" and "human capital." These expenses, gone unchecked, can cripple our organizations. Much time and consideration must be given to hiring. The first step to bringing in key people is to *evaluate what you are good at and what you are not so good at.*

Most people stop there, but I am going to share with you a level-up secret: Include what you don't like to do. Sometimes you are good at something, but you don't like doing it. There are two things you, as the leader, should never let go of completely—the checkbook and sales/marketing.

Remember, the basic formula for success is Revenue - Expenses = Profit. That is, revenue (sales and marketing) must exceed expenses (checkbook) to create profit (success). You may not be completely hands-on in these areas, but you must certainly be hands in. Everything else needs to be evaluated, factoring in *what you like to do.*

Many leaders do not realize the long-term negative effect that doing things you hate to do has on your vision and creativity. Time is zero-sum, so don't forget about the things in your personal life that can help free up time.

Once you've made a thorough assessment of your time, you will begin to see what's needed to help you focus on what only you can do. Usually, the first hire needs to be an assistant—personal, executive, or a combination of both. Don't be afraid to have your personal assistant address areas of both your business/ministry life and your personal life. Again, time is a zero-sum game, and if you find someone who does not want to help you in whatever area is needed, then you have the wrong person. I hope this goes without saying, but I am going to mention it anyway. *As long as it is legal, moral, and ethical, your assistant should be willing to take the burden off your shoulders so that you can do what only YOU can do.*

Next comes the second hire, the person who can take the things you outsource and save you money by getting them done internally, and vice versa. It's a better investment to hire outside contractors on some things. For example, if you spend all night preparing the books and crunching numbers, you may be better off hiring a bookkeeper. That person may charge you a higher hourly rate, but they will be able to accomplish what takes you five hours to do in one hour.

As you develop your hiring plan, know that it's not "one size fits all." Your plan is idiosyncratic, that is, unique to your business and your needs. All of which must be assessed before the water starts to boil. The problem is that when the pressure comes, and the water begins to boil, most of us will hire to the pain and not to plan

Assess what you are good at and hire staff to accommodate your weaknesses. One of the things I always need to remember is that there is always somebody out there who plays at what I hate—in other words, someone who finds peace and joy in doing the things I hate to do. Take the time to find that person.

Proverbs 26:10 (CSB) says, "The one who hires a fool or who hires those passing by is like an archer who wounds everyone." If you don't take the time to find the right person for the right place, you'll "wound everyone."

Lastly, remember to *keep your hiring practices geared toward revenue creation and not just support and administration.* Sometimes the admin and support are the most pressing need—the squeaky wheel. Leaders often tend toward hiring people who mirror their strengths. But never forget, you'll have nothing to service if you don't have new sales or clients. And people who can sell it are not always the people who can do it. Remember the old saying, "Those who can't do, teach." And the money that allows them not to do it and teach it is generated by those who can sell it.

To recap:
- Number One: Develop a plan (Spend the time; I can't stress this enough).
- Number Two: Hire a personal or executive assistant.
- Number Three: Outsource or insource to create maximum efficiencies.
- Number Four: Hire more front-end revenue-generating people than admin people.

Reflection

1. Quick Summary

2. Key Insights

3. Personal Application

4. Meaningful Quotes

WEEK 33

Training People to Be Nice

Whenever I go to Starbucks, I am amazed at their baristas' ability to serve their customers. They tend to be very energetic and polite. It's often had me wondering if they are eating their own cooking. Are they hyped on the coffee, so to speak? And at Chick-fil-A, the people are so nice and friendly. I'm amazed at the level of care people can provide when it is one of the values of their organization.

How do you get people to pay $5 for coffee that costs you 15 cents? When all the costs are factored in, how would you like to have a margin of profit of 80%? Well, I am going to reveal the strategy straight from the playbook of high-performance organizations.

There is a saying, "No good thing cheap and no cheap thing good." In today's culture, a smiling face and a soothing voice have been replaced with an informal email, a chat bot, or a person who looks at you as if you are interfering with their day—while they are at work.

One of the biggest problems inevitably faced by every business and ministry as they grow and expand is that they have to rely upon people to help. An African Proverb says, "If you want to go fast, go alone. If you want to go far, go together." If you can accomplish your dream by yourself and without people, then I assure you that you do not have a God-sized dream. If your vision is not intimidating to you, then it is likely insulting to God.

The challenge as your organization grows and expands is to find people who will represent you correctly. A few years ago, my mentor told me this story. He had told one of his kids to go get his sister and tell her to come downstairs. The sibling ran upstairs and, with all the sternness and frustration he could muster, barked out, "Dad wants you downstairs right now, and you're in trouble!"

The issue was, that wasn't the case, and the child was misrepresenting the parent. We have to be careful because, oftentimes, we can hire people who might misrepresent us for a myriad of reasons. They don't have radical ownership, so the outcome doesn't matter to them. Maybe they have your hands—they are skilled and talented—but they don't have your heart.

While I do not believe that the customer is "always" right, I do believe that you are to "always" be respectful.

Proverbs 15:1 says, "A gentle answer turns away wrath, but a harsh word stirs up anger."

Customer service is a lost art. I am almost always disappointed with the low level of service companies provide. I remember dining at certain restaurants and being impressed with their level of service; now it feels like a money grab.

We tend to underestimate the impact that people who work with us and/or for us have on an organization. A few years back, I went to a restaurant where the maître d' was an older woman who was extremely rude. I am not one to leave bad reviews publicly because I don't want to tarnish an organization's reputation over one incident. There are always times when anyone can miss it. So, I asked for the owner and explained what happened. I was met with a shrug and that was the end of it. Still reeling from the experience, I went online and began to prepare my review. I had deemed that since the owner didn't seem to care, then I would do my public duty to warn people. Much to my surprise, there were already several reviews complaining about this woman. I was shocked as to why she would be allowed to continue in her position until I read that she was the owner's mother. Nepotism at its finest.

Author Jeff Hyman is quoted as saying, "Ninety percent of business problems are recruiting problems in disguise."[53]

See, your members, your customers, your clients, your donors, or your supporters —whatever you call them in your organization—will never be happier than your employees.

Famous and yet infamous billionaire hotelier Leona Helmsley was quoted saying, "At my hotel, you receive sincere attention not synthetic smiles. I don't hire people who have to be told to be nice. I hire nice people." Interestingly enough, she herself was dubbed "the queen of mean." Even if you are not the most personable, you must be mindful of hiring people who are.

Bruce Nordstrom likes to say, "We can hire nice people and teach them to sell, but we can't hire salespeople and teach them to be nice."

I read an article about Chick-fil-A that said they "don't train people to be nice. [They] make it central to the interview process to recruit nice people."

You can't train people to be nice. Some people have a face for radio—they need to be in the back end of the organization, behind the scenes or not at all. Many of the problems we experience within organizations are really people problems and not business problems. Your business may be great, but you have people in the front office who act like they are sucking on lemons all day.

---

[53] Hyman, J. D. Recruit Rockstars: the 10 Step Playbook to Find the Winners and Ignite Your Business. Lioncrest Publishing, 2018.

Reflection

1. Quick Summary

2. Key Insights

3. Personal Application

4. Meaningful Quotes

WEEK 34

Delegation: The Magic Bullet - Part 1

I have to admit that even I can struggle with delegation. Oftentimes, the business and the "overwhelm" can get the best of you. If there were any magic bullets to leadership, delegation would definitely be at the top of my list.

Leaders can tend to avoid delegation because, well, let's face it, in your mind, nobody can do this better than you can. Or you might think, it'll take more time to explain it to someone else than it does for you to just jump on it and git-r done.

These may be true if you are shortsighted, but to be the leader God called you to be, you will find that you must begin to kick the can further down the road and prepare now for all that is about to come. It is a principle of spiritual readiness.

Remember to be creative in your delegation. Sometimes you can limit your thinking and not realize that even if you are a "solo-prenuer," there are many creative ways to delegate. You may or may not have an assistant. But there may be a volunteer who can take on those responsibilities. You may be able to hire a professional for a contract rate that may be a little more expensive than you'd like, but the value they will bring long-term is exponential.

Habakkuk 2:2 says, "Write the vision, and make it plain upon tables, that he may run that readeth it."

This scripture is full of nuggets, one of which is the fact that whatever the total vision is, it will take more than you to accomplish.

Always remember that if you can accomplish the vision by yourself, then it is likely that it is not a God vision. No matter how you slice it, you need people to accomplish the vision, whether they are employees or volunteer servers. You, as a leader, must master the critical Art of Delegation. Delegation will free you up to do what only you can do, thereby exponentially growing your capacity. Delegation will pay for itself in the long run if you are patient and stay the course.

I believe volumes of books could be written on this subject, but my goal here is to give you a high-level actionable overview.

Your first step in delegation is *determining what to delegate and to whom*. The issue of *to whom* is preceded by the *what*, so we will begin there.

You will need to take a moment and think through a few areas of your business or ministry. You'll need to *make a list of what tasks you do that only you can do*. This is your sweet spot. This is a place of decision—where you are in control and directing your success. These are things that only you can and should do. These are the things that "ring the bell," "make it rain," or grow the business. In other words, what are your most critical functions?

I call these *The 3C's: Content, Casting, and Clarity*.

Since my most important functions are writing and speaking, my primary functions (the *Content*) include creating sermons and material for podcasts, books, our website, videos, and the like. My second priority is *Casting* the vision internally within our organization, then externally, that is, marketing. My final priority is *Clarity* —seeking to find places within my organization that lack clarity and then determine how to bring that clarity. In the Bible, James 3:16 tells us that wherever there is strife, there is confusion and every evil work.

Once you've defined your three priorities, they determine your "Do" category. This is what you keep and never delegate in its entirety to someone else. As your business or ministry evolves, your priorities may evolve with it, but you never delegate that which only you should do.

All you super achievers need to understand this key principle—I urge you to hear this and hear it well. *Good to Great* author Jim Collins said, "If you have more than three priorities, *you don't have any*."

What does that mean to you? Everything else needs to be delegated. You should be looking to mercilessly trim your list down to what only you can do.

If you do this correctly, you will have a long list of tasks that need to be delegated. I am going to help you navigate that list as well. But for now, I want you to take this really seriously. Please! This is critical because the rest of this process is going to be built on the shoulders of this task. It will require your total focus. If you don't invest the time, you will be throwing good after bad, so make the investment. It will truly be worth it.

Week 34: Delegation - The Magic Bullet, Part 1

Reflection

1. Quick Summary

2. Key Insights

3. Personal Application

4. Meaningful Quotes

WEEK 35

Delegation: The Magic Bullet - Part 2

Often, emerging leaders ask if there is a magic bullet to leadership. The short answer is no. But if anything comes close to being a magic bullet, it's delegation.

I previously mentioned Habakkuk 2:2, to make the vision plain so that someone who reads it may run to help you accomplish it. It will take more than you alone to accomplish the vision.

A true "God vision" will be one you cannot accomplish by yourself. No matter how you slice it, you need people (whether employees or volunteers) to accomplish the vision. As a leader, you must master the art of delegation, which will free you up to do what only you can, and exponentially grow your capacity. It will pay for itself in the long run.

Remember, the *first thing* you must do is *determine what to delegate and to whom*.

By now, you should have spent some time creating a journal of everything you do. If your list is very short, then there are two things you may need to understand. One, you were not thorough in really keeping track of everything you do. Please be mindful that many things you do are *in the mastery zone* for you and are *almost done on autopilot*, so it really is imperative that you think it completely through and from the eyes of an outsider and not autopilot. Two, maybe you really aren't doing anything, and you must find better ways to manage your time and increase your workload.

From that list, you should have refined it down to your top three—and only three. Remember, if you have more than three priorities, you don't have any. This list needs to include what only you should do, and more importantly, what only you can do. This is your sweet spot, your place of decision—where you take charge, control, and direct your success. In my case, it's the *3C's of Content, Casting, and Clarity*.

Once you have figured out your big three, then the rest of the list needs to be sorted into other categories. These are: (1) The Drudgery List, (2) The Distraction List, and (3) The Delusion List.

The first category is the Drudgery List. These are things *that must get done*, but you may or may not be proficient in them; more importantly, *you hate doing them*. They steal your emotional energy and sap your zeal. Never forget: There are people who play at what you consider drudgery. These are the first items for you to delegate.

Second is the Distraction List. These are the things you do to distract yourself from doing what's important. You know how you have that big important thing to do, so you sit down and check/respond to your email, and at the end of the day, you haven't accomplished the most important thing. Or you are constantly answering your phone whenever it rings because you've been "Pavlov-ed" to believe every phone call is important. Then you come to the end of your day, and nothing else has gotten done. The truth of the matter is that answering every phone call is a distraction, a way of avoiding the important work you must do. These distractions comprise the second list of things you need to delegate.

The third list is the Delusion List. These are things that you think you're good at, but in reality, there are much more qualified people who can accomplish them. This will likely become a list of things that only contractors and professionals can do. Listen, I know you love tinkering with your website, but there are many more qualified people out there to do that (unless websites are your business). I think you get my point. You may be great at bookkeeping, but hiring a bookkeeper is certainly better than staying up all night trying the cook the books while burning the midnight oil. You can spend hours doing what a professional (e.g., an attorney, an accountant, a bookkeeper) can accomplish in a fraction of the time.

Take time this week to finalize your task list. This must be well thought-through, so take the time to get it clear. Next, I'll cover the "HOW" of Delegation.

Week 35: Delegation - The Magic Bullet - Part 2

Reflection

1. Quick Summary

2. Key Insights

3. Personal Application

4. Meaningful Quotes

WEEK 36

Delegation: The Magic Bullet - Part 3

Now that you have all your tasks listed and categorized, you should have a master list of all these tasks sorted into four categories.
- Your Do category, which is your primary and vital functions.
- Your Drudgery List, the things that you hate to do but need to be done.
- Your Distraction List, things you use to avoid meaningful work you need to do.
- Your Delusion List, things a professional can do better or faster than you.

As you look through these lists, you will probably see many things that you realize should not be done at all. You should add those items to a fifth list that you toss into the garbage can.

All these lists may appear to be daunting, but let's break them down into manageable portions.

First, you begin delegating items from the Drudgery List. These sap your energy and steal your joy, and you want to get them off your plate ASAP. As you get rid of these things, you will be more creative and have more margin in your life to evaluate and solve the real problems your organization has. Your kids, your spouse, and your family will recognize how much happier you are when you rid yourself of these drains on your productivity.

After you have successfully cleared the Drudgery List, you should move on to the Distraction List. This one is a little harder because it tends to become the crutch on which you have relied in an unhealthy way. The Distraction List is what you use to convince yourself that you are busy, often using these things to escape from the real focal points of business, career, or ministry.

Once much of that is gone, you will be forced to face what is important. You also may have to deal with your self-image and not be scared that you are somehow rendering yourself useless by delegating. Remember, no one can do what you do. The Bible tells us that you were fearfully and wonderfully made. No one can ever replace you, so you are not creating job security by holding on to everything. You must learn to "quit your way to the top" and find others to do what you can but don't need to do to climb the ladder.

It is pretty much impossible to promote someone out of a position that only they know how to do.

If you have effectively delegated the first two lists, you will find that your income has increased exponentially or, at minimum, you can see that it will soon. Now you can afford to deal with the last category—Delusion. These are things the professionals can do in a fraction of the time it takes for you to do them. For example, my hourly worth is well over a hundred dollars an hour. To have my car detailed takes four hours and costs me $150. Even if I could do it as fast as the professional car washer can (which, I assure you, I can't), at minimum it would cost me $400-worth of my time (or, realistically, more like $600). For me, this is like buying back time. Now, if you do this sort of thing for pleasure and enjoyment, then go for it. But you must be merciless about recovering time to work on the most important things.

Here is the inside scoop on how to get all this delegating done. Let's discuss the Five Levels of Delegation. There is a huge difference between abdication and delegation. These Five Levels of Delegation offer a standardized language for you and your team to begin understanding the nuances of delegating. It is important to the outcome that when something is delegated, people (1) know what the expectation is, and (2) have agreed upon the intended outcome in advance. This will save you quite a bit of frustration in the long run.

Level 1 Delegation: *Do exactly what I say*. This means just what it says—do exactly what I have asked you to do. Don't deviate from my instructions. I have already researched the options and determined what I want you to do. This is the lowest level of delegation and merely a request for obedience to the specific task or request

Level 2 Delegation: *Research and report*. This means to research the topic, gather information, and report what you discover. We will discuss it, and then I will make the decision and tell you what I want you to do.

This is your first opportunity to assess a person's ability to do research. This is a vital step to training people so that they don't have to be micro-managed. At this stage, the results of their research will help you to understand a few things:
1. Will they do the heavy lifting?
2. Do they have a firm understanding of what you have asked them to do?
3. It helps them to learn the why behind your decision-making.

Level 3 Delegation: *Research and recommend*. This means to research, outline a minimum of three options, and bring your best recommendation. Give me the pros and cons of each option, then tell me what you think we should do. If I agree, I will authorize you to move forward. If I don't agree, I will offer you a better solution.

This level gives you insight into their decision-making skills and allows you to assess and speak into their decision making, thus allowing you to train them to think and decide as you do. You want to hear the details of their decision-making process, so you can understand why they chose their recommendation. At times, they may have a better and more ingenious idea. Other times, they will have missed the mark completely. Again, it is critical to understand that you are stepping people through this process to train them to reach the ultimate level of trust, which is a Level 5 delegation. The speed by which people ascend the levels will be up to them. It is completely dependent on how fast they can catch on. And always remember that people can have different competencies, so the rate of their ascension can change based on the nature of the task.

Level 4 Delegation: *Decide and inform*. This means they should make a decision and then tell me what they did. I trust them to do the research, make the best decision they can, and then keep me in the loop. I don't want to be surprised.

Again, at this level, you are creating a level of transparency and accountability, but you trust that they can make the right decision. You may have a project you are working on that depends on the outcome of a certain task. You will need to know what the outcome is to move forward.

Level 5 Delegation (the highest level of delegation): *Just handle it*. This means you want them to make whatever decision they think is best—no need to report back. You're saying to them, "I trust you completely. I know you will follow through. You have my full support."

This highest level of delegation requires the least amount of supervision and eliminates the need for micro-management of your people.

Most of the time, you will start with Level 1 and allow trust and competency to be established. As you continue to grow in your management of your people, you will find that most of your people will grow in their execution as the overall level of competency grows.

Your next homework assignment is to begin this process on some of your tasks. Next, we will discuss where to find people to delegate to and some of the traps to avoid as you go through this process. I am going to share some tips that I, unfortunately, learned the hard way, and they will help you avoid some of the costly mistakes that I have made.

Reflection

1. Quick Summary

2. Key Insights

3. Personal Application

4. Meaningful Quotes

WEEK 37

Delegation: The Magic Bullet - Part 4

Previously, we talked about the key skill of delegation and why it is so important. We also discussed a method of prioritizing and organizing everything you do in preparation for delegating all—and I mean all—non-essential tasks.

Next, we discussed how to standardize the delegation process and to create a language and communication that will allow for effective delegation as well as training those you manage to grow in their skill and trust.

So, who are the people you can delegate to? Let's start with the obvious pool—your assistant and/or your employees. I don't think we need to spend too much time on this, but one word of caution: *Be careful not to dump too much too fast.* Remember, you probably have been doing a certain task for a while, and they have not. So, you must be mindful of a certain learning curve.

The second pool is made up of volunteers. You may have people in your employ or ministry who are willing to help and assist you. They may not be able to take on the whole task, but they could feasibly start with a piece of it, and as they demonstrate greater commitment and skill, you can increase their involvement and role. You will be surprised how many people who are serving around you are willing to help alleviate the pressure.

The final people to whom you may delegate are the professionals. Ask your peers for recommendations of service providers such as accountants, attorneys, and others who can take on some of the load for a nominal fee.

Once you have developed your cadre of support, here a few common pitfalls to avoid:

1. *Fuzzy communication* We sometimes think our communication is clear when it really isn't. We have a term that we use in our organizations—CECO, that is, *communicate early and communicate often*. As aggravating as it may be at times, you must over-communicate to ensure that people understand not only the "what" but also the "why." This will alleviate frustration in the long run.

2. *Uncommunicated Expectations* Common sense is really not that common. When dealing with delegation, people tend to assume that certain things are just "understood." If you don't have a clear expectation of both the "what" of your task but also the "why" and the "how," you need to know it is probably not ready to be delegated. You must be able to articulate your expectations clearly or a lot of trial and error will occur, unfortunately, at your expense.

3. *Abdication* Delegation is not abdication. When you abdicate the task, there tends to be little to no follow-up or investment. On the other hand, if you delegate it,

you must build in a mechanism to follow up and stay connected to its outcome (unless it is a Level 5). Otherwise, the task requires some level of accountability and reporting, whether through project-management software or regular meetings (virtual or in-person) with updates. People don't do what you *expect*; they do what you *inspect*.

If you work to avoid these common pitfalls, you will find that you can become a delegation ninja. It is not easy, but it is truly *the superpower of the elite*.

A final thought: As tedious as this may sound, delegation is the one skill I implore you to master. It will pay great dividends in the end and become the source code to your success.

Reflection

1. Quick Summary

2. Key Insights

3. Personal Application

4. Meaningful Quotes

WEEK 38

Being the Guide

Most movies have three central characters, the hero, the enigmatic/wise guide, and the villain. The hero tends to make some great transitional growth or revelation by the end of the movie after having arrived at this place with the help of the guide. Luke Skywalker had Yoda. In *The Matrix,* Neo had Morpheus. In *Silence of the Lambs*, Clarice had Hannibal Lector. The list goes on and on.

Organizations miss the crux of effective market positioning because they try to position themselves as the hero. In a consumer's story, there is room for only one hero, and, of course, in their minds, they are it. *Your organization is not the hero.* They are. Who is "they"? The people, the clients, the customers, those you serve. They should be the hero; your organization is merely the guide. Thus, you have to establish the leader of your organization as one who is worthy of taking the position of the Wise Guide in the stories of your clients' lives.

While I watch many organizations try to lead by committee, I don't see that pattern reflected biblically. God had a one-man plan. Many leaders in the Bible were individually needed to make the ultimate decision, and they did so at times with the counsel of wise people, but their leadership was not by committee. We don't need a group of five people to determine what toilet paper to put in the bathroom.

I am about to enter a potentially slippery slope, and I want you to please understand where I am going with this. Jesus is, in fact, our all in all. And our overall goal/vision/service has to always be about Him. You are, however, integral to the success of the organization, and people must buy into you as the leader. I want to reiterate that *it is all about Jesus.* But all of the body universally has Jesus as their Chief Shepherd; if He is all that is needed to lead His Church, why do some organizations and churches succeed and others fail? Sometimes the narrow focus of the overly spiritual misses the idea that while it is all about Jesus, we are still dealing with people, and we must understand how to reach them effectively.

If we are not careful, we can downplay our involvement and role in the success of the organizations God has entrusted us with.

We have to be mindful of the fact that, while we need good (solid, mature, talented) people around us, the success of our organization and, dare I say, "brand" hinges upon us individually and personally being established and credible. God told Abraham that He would make his name great. That was because He trusted that Abraham would make His name known. See, *God's name is already great. We need to make Him known.* Some in the Christian community balk at secular terms like "branding." The Bible says Jesus' fame went out into society (Matthew 4:24; Mark

1:28; Luke 4:27). In reality, that was marketing—word-of-mouth marketing, to be exact.

As you establish your business or ministry, you must fully and humbly understand that one of the keys to success rises and falls on your ability to present the leader as an authority. People need a face and a credible person to connect with. While we are certainly trying to connect people with Jesus, we must understand that humans, by nature, only connect with humans—at least, initially. Many of us, as leaders, are the face of our organizations. This is why many organizations have a spokesperson—i.e. a face. Understanding this takes a certain amount of maturity. Some people see this as self-aggrandizement; it is not. The Apostle Paul told people to follow him as he follows Christ.

You will have to take the time to become *the authority* in your area. There are a few effective ways to do that.

One is to *compile and report industry trends, developments, and forecasts*. There are many details related to your profession and/or industry. If you take the time to thoughtfully curate and then disseminate them, you will establish yourself as an authority in your field.

Two, *write white papers, articles, blogs*, depending on what's appropriate. Do workshops and seminars, radio segments, speaking engagements for local organizations. These are all effective ways to establish yourself in the marketplace.

Three, *write a book*! Leaders often miss and underutilize this opportunity because it continues to carry a certain mystique of difficulty and inaccessibility to the "common man."

But a book can position you in a market and be one of your most effective branding tools.

I have a very dear friend who is a Messianic rabbi, Dr. Allan Moorhead. He wrote a book called *The Coming Captivity and Restoration of Israel*. It's an excellent book, and I recommend you pick up a copy. However, that book ended up in the hands of a worldwide missionary, and Dr. Moorhead has subsequently been invited overseas several times and taught in several countries, including Turkey, Israel, and a few African nations.

See! A book has the ability to establish you as an authority. It also has the ability to open doors for you. It can go further than you can in your current sphere of influence. It is amazing how many doors of ministry and opportunity were opened worldwide because one book fell into the hands of someone whom the author did not initially know, and it opened a great and effectual door of opportunity for him.

Look at how many leaders have great books under their belts to establish and brand themselves for the growth of the organizations they lead.

Jack Welch wrote *Winning*; Donald Trump co-authored *Trump: The Art of the Deal*; Bill Gates wrote *Business @ The Speed of Thought*. You are the expert on your vision, and you must understand how to leverage that into an advantage and worldwide positioning.

Week 38: Being the Guide

Many people who self-publish a book try to find the cheapest way to make it happen, not realizing that your book is the first impression you will make on the public. People will see your book before they see you. It needs to be professional and high quality. Unfortunately, self-publishing companies have deluded authors wanting to enter the book world with tons of low-quality books.

Here is a quick tip for you. One of the most common mistakes writers make when they self-publish—and I mean COMMON—is putting the word "forward" at the top of their book's introductory remarks. Forward means "to advance." It is not the same thing as the FOREWORD, meaning the "before word" in a book. This common mistake is a telltale sign of a low-quality book.

A couple of years ago, I presented a seminar on publishing, which I recently had transcribed. I am willing to release the transcription to you under two conditions:

One, you understand that it is a manuscript that has not yet been fully edited and developed, so that needs to be taken into consideration, but the material is all there, and it's very helpful.

Two, you don't share it with anyone.

If you would like a copy of this transcript, you can join our Facebook group, #LEVELUP, for this and more free resources.

Despite the obvious fact that a book (if handled correctly) will create another profit center to help fund the work you do, it can also be a great door opener as a giveaway to attract new customers, members, and donors. It paves the way to speaking engagements. If handled well, your book becomes a great tool to help grow and establish your business or ministry.

Here is another key point: If you are a speaker or minister, *you already have an immense library of great content.* Full disclosure here, but one of my companies is a Christian boutique book publisher that specializes in helping Christian leaders communicate their message to the world. Unlike many "vanity presses," our company has *the ability to develop the manuscript for you from audio or video recordings.*

As for me, I am not so good at sitting down and staring at a cursor on a blank screen to start typing out a book. But I am gifted at speaking. One of the keys to my success at prolifically cranking out books—11 to be exact—is this ability to have my spoken sermons turned into manuscripts that I can edit into what I want, as opposed to starting from scratch with the written word. If you would like more information about publishing your next book, you can visit www.aionmultimedia.com.

Whatever method you choose, remember the world needs what is inside of you. You are a fountain of knowledge and revelation and a catalyst to transformation. Don't bury it, but allow your gift to make room for you.

Reflection

1. Quick Summary

2. Key Insights

3. Personal Application

4. Meaningful Quotes

WEEK 39

The Art of the Pivot

Winston Churchill, one of the greatest leaders of all-time, famously said, "Never give in—never, never, never, never—in nothing, great or small, large or petty—never give in except to convictions of honor and good sense."[54]

I admire Churchill, but one of this generation's greatest prophets, Kenny Rogers, offered great wisdom when he sang, "You've got to know when to hold 'em, know when to fold 'em, know when to walk away, know when to run."[55]

In the proper context, ambition can be a blessing, but in the wrong context, it can be a curse. In Mark 8:36, Jesus poses the question, "For what shall it profit a man, if he shall gain the whole world, and lose his own soul?"

Sometimes in the pursuit of becoming bigger, we really don't become better—just bigger. People can have an unquenchable desire for more and not a desire to be more effective, or more prolific or even to have a greater impact. Subsequently, all that growth does is create more headaches, more problems; it pulls you away from your family only to realize that you are not creating the result you once desired.

After Steve Jobs was ousted from Apple in 1985, he started a high-performance computer manufacturing company called NeXT Computers. He bought Pixar (then known as Graphics Group) from Lucasfilm for 5 million dollars. It was part of Lucasfilm's computer division. Their goal with NeXT was to build supercomputers that would be able to create animated graphics at lightning speed—something that had never been done before. They sold only 100 of them and eventually decided to sell off the hardware part and focus on making films. *Toy Story* was the first-ever fully computer-animated movie of its kind. The *Toy Story* franchise has grossed 1.9 billion dollars worldwide. Jobs became the company's largest shareholder and was CEO until Disney bought it for $7.4 billion in 2006.

Jobs recognized the opportunity and *pivoted*. As a result, he turned a 5-million-dollar investment into a 7.4-billion-dollar return. He went in with the expectation of building supercomputers and realized the *opportunity within the opportunity* was making animated films.[56]

---

[54] "Never Give In, Never, Never, Never, 1941." *America's National Churchill Museum*, www.nationalchurchillmuseum.org/never-give-in-never-never-never.html.

[55] Rogers, Kenny. "The Gambler." *The Gambler*, Don Schlitz, Dream Catcher, 1978, Song Facts, www.songfacts.com/lyrics/kenny-rogers/the-gambler

[56] *Steve Jobs*. 10 June 2020, www.biography.com/business-figure/steve-jobs.

Even if you have spent good money, be careful not to spend good money after bad.

Never be afraid to pivot. Sometimes people can become so pedantic and focused that they miss the cues to pivot. Sometimes what you are doing gets you into the right area, but you are on the wrong street. An old saying goes, "You are in the right church, just sitting on the wrong pew." I am not telling you to drop what you're doing altogether, but you may need to pivot.

Reflection

1. Quick Summary

2. Key Insights

3. Personal Application

4. Meaningful Quotes

WEEK 40

Not If You Mess Up, But When

What should you do, *not if, but when* you mess up? I have seen many leaders try the ostrich effect when it comes to mistakes. They will bury their head in the sand and act as if nothing has occurred. They feel the guilt of their mistakes and assume that people know what is going on inside them. Trust me, people do not know what's happening inside you, and this behavior causes more harm than good. I have had employees who have made major mess-ups (that I ultimately have had to bear the brunt of), and there was little to no apology or thank you, or, for that matter, any level of acknowledgment of their mistake. As if appreciation and thanks can go unspoken yet, somehow, be understood.

Our society seems to be developing people who don't understand social etiquette. I have noticed this in particular with the younger generations. The truth is, we all make mistakes, but to ignore them or act as if they haven't happened does way more damage to relationships than people know. Some years ago, very early in my career, I was on a call with a vendor. They were giving me a hard time, and I hit what I thought was the mute button, making some not-so-nice comments about the individual's IQ on the other end of the line. When I realized that I, in fact, had not hit the mute button, I was horrified, and frankly, so was the person on the other end. Inevitably, you will make a mistake. When you do, I assure you that you can recover from it if you handle it well. It takes twelve positive experiences to make up for one unresolved negative experience—so it is worth the time and effort to make it right.

While I don't believe the adage that the customer is always right, I do believe that *the customer is always to be valued and respected*. I call it the Golden Rule. That certainly includes doing unto others as you would have them do unto you, but I am referring specifically to another version: *He who has the gold makes the rules.* Your customer has the gold and is risking their gold to do business with you. You owe them a fiduciary responsibility of *Care, Obedience, Accountability, Loyalty, and Disclosure.* According to statistics, people tell 50% more people about a bad experience than a good one.

You have to be mindful of the difference between a customer and a client. A client is one who is *under the care of another.* When you see people—even vendors, employers, employees—as clients, it garners a greater sense of responsibility toward them.

Maybe you messed up in a certain situation and received a bad review online. Let's face it; we all mess up at times. Fifty-one percent of people will not do business with you again after one bad experience. Therefore, I would say that it is probably very important how you handle people with whom you mess up.

Now, I am going to help you with how to respond to your *faux pas*.

Step One: Run to the battle quickly. Anger is always a secondary emotion. If people are upset with you, it's usually rooted in their feeling disrespected. If trust has been breached, people often respond better when they know you've made them a priority and see you rushing to resolve the situation.

Step Two: Don't ignore your blunder. And don't try to defend or justify it. Trying to explain or justify your mistake becomes very ego-driven. The truth of the matter is that no-one cares about your excuses. That's just the honest truth.

You must take responsibility and own your mistake. Have you ever heard of the ADD tactic: *Admit* nothing; *Deny* everything; *Demand* proof?

That strategy doesn't work in business. *Admit* and *apologize* and then go to step number three, the most important step in the process:

Step Three (and, I repeat, this is the *most important step* in the process): *Chase their respect*. Figure out ways to overdo it.

In the situation I mentioned earlier, I sent a huge bouquet of flowers and a card and an email, and I apologized via phone and in person. Upon being profusely apologetic, my apology was accepted, and I gained a great ally. Our future business dealings were unbelievably easy, and the vendor I insulted went far above and beyond to help my company win in any way possible. I gained an advocate. Often, your worst mess-ups can lead to your greatest successes.

Especially remember, if you get a bad review, to post all of these facts on the review. Eighty percent of people who are trying to decide whether to deal with you will research you online and will immediately gravitate to the bad reviews. They are interested in how you handle the problems and not just the ones who sing your praises.

Advanced Tip! When you have turned the situation around, don't forget to ask them if they would up their rating or modify their review. Always ask!

To recap:

1. Run to the battle. Urgency communicates importance.
2. Admit and Apologize.
3. Most importantly: Chase their respect. Overdo it.

Reflection

1. Quick Summary

2. Key Insights

3. Personal Application

4. Meaningful Quotes

WEEK 41

5 Keys to a Wealthy Mindset

Babies typically enter the world at birth headfirst. If they are not situated that way in the womb, the doctor tries their best to turn at baby around in utero to get the proper positioning before dropping into the birth canal.

So it is with your mind. Everywhere you go in life, you will go head first. If you free your mind, the rest of you will follow.

The Bible tells us in Proverbs 23:7, "As a man thinketh in his heart, so is he."

We must understand the power of strongholds. Without getting into a Bible college lesson, I want you to understand that, biblically, you are never told to cast *out* a stronghold but to cast it *down*. A stronghold is really a flaw in one's thinking that needs to be changed. Many do not even realize that a *poverty mindset is a precursor to a poverty spirit*.

So here are *the first three of six mind shifts* you must make in order to become wealthy. And by "wealthy," I do not just mean moneywise, but I'm talking about having a *full supply in every area of your life*.

#1 Do you need quick gratification?

In other words, does present pleasure mean more to you than future gain? If so, you will have to learn *the art of the long view*. Patience is truly a virtue, and many people have no idea how close they are to their breakthroughs before they give up. *Consistency and constancy are key.* So is *delayed gratification*. In our LeaderSHIFT Success Masterclass, we discuss the principle that one of the greatest indications of success is the ability to delay gratification.

In the 1960s, Stanford psychology professor Walter Mischel studied the effects of delayed gratification in preschool-aged children using marshmallows and other treats. He and his team would put a child in a room and offer them one marshmallow. If they could sit in the room with the marshmallow for a specified period of time without eating it, they would receive another treat. They learned that the kids who could resist the temptation to gobble up the marshmallow immediately and delay gratification later fared better in school and in life over the course of thirty years.[57] *Your ability to delay gratification is essential to your overall success.*

#2 Do you have shallow networking relationships?

---

[57] Suttie, Jill. "Kids Do Better on the Marshmallow Test When They Cooperate." *Greater Good*, 2020, greatergood.berkeley.edu/article/item/kids_do_better_on_the_marshmallow_test_when_they_cooperate.

There is often a temptation to go wide and not deep. Trust me—it is a fatal flaw. I spoke with a contractor who went to a networking meeting where he met a young man who was energetically "working the room," getting as many business cards as possible—going wide instead of deep. The contractor explained how disinterested he was in doing business with this guy and how his way of accumulating contacts was actually a turnoff. People don't care how much you know until they know how much you care. Take the time to develop deeper relationships. Zig Ziglar said it best: "You can have everything in life you want if you will just help other people get what they want." Take the time to go deep and not settle for shallow volume. Dig the wells of interest and purposeful value in your relationships and see what kind of results you get.

#3 Do you have a plan?

If you fail to plan, you are planning to fail. Put a strategy down on paper. As you being to write, you will notice a few things: *Clarity* will come, and things that are *unclear* in your mind will become *even more unclear* on paper. According to leadership expert Peter Economy (Yes, his name really is Peter Economy—I checked), "You are 42 percent more likely to achieve your goals if you write them down. Writing your goals down not only forces you to get clear on what, exactly, it is that you want to accomplish, but doing so plays a part in motivating you to complete the tasks necessary for your success." Take the time to write down your plan and keep the vision in front of you. Remember, the Bible says, "Write the vision; make it plain so that those who read it may run."

Making these shifts is a challenge, but I assure you, if you make them, you will be well on your way to building through wealth.

Reflection

1. Quick Summary

2. Key Insights

3. Personal Application

4. Meaningful Quotes

WEEK 42

5 Keys to a Wealthy Mindset - Part 2

Here is the continuation of the six mind shifts from the previous chapter that you must make in order to become wealthy. I am not just talking about money but also those who have a full supply in every area of their life.

#4 Do the people around you support your goals?

If people around you think your ideas are ridiculous, then you need a new peer group. Many studies show that one of the greatest influences on your success is the quality of the peer group around you. It can be said that you are the sum of your five closest friends. I remember hearing a story about Kenneth Hagin Sr. when asked about why he had wealthy people on his board. He said it was because they don't flinch when you have to do large projects and things that cost big money. Your dreams may not be too big in your mind—they are just too big for your smaller-minded friends. Eagle don't hang with chickens. I think you get the point.

#5 Do you need to look successful now?

Many people short-circuit their success over the desire to *look successful* rather than *be successful*. "Authenticity" is the name of the game, not "keeping up with the Joneses." The Bible says that those who compare themselves among themselves are not wise (2 Cor. 10:12). Do you find yourself needing to appear a certain way? You will have to *forego the appearance of success*; keep your head down and *become successful*. If you have to *show* and *tell* everyone that you are in charge, then, in all likelihood, you are not in charge. Keeping up an image can become a fulltime job. I have seen people lose focus on what's important because they are tending to the irrelevant while keeping up appearances.

#6 Do you only save or do you only earn?

You will never save your way to wealth. Many people have a stingy spirit and are just plain poverty-minded. They think they can save their way to wealth, but that is not possible. Others frivolously spend their money thinking they can always earn more.

There is a balance between saving and earning. The book of Proverbs speaks of the ant that works and stores; it says that the ant is wise. The message there is that you must earn first and save second. This is a common misconnect that the wealthy have overcome. One of the greatest misconceptions is that there is a direct connection between money and time. There isn't. Jeff Bezos makes $2,500 per second.[58] That means if he dropped a 100-dollar bill, trying to pick it up would cost him more than it's worth. Time is the great leveler. Bezos has the exact same amount of time that you and I have. We have to break free from the 9-to-5 mentality we've learned that says there is a direct connection between money and time that does not exist. Money can be earned in little to no time as long as time is invested and not spent.

Making these shifts is a challenge, but I assure you, if you make them, you will be well on your way to building wealth. We don't want wealth for the sake of personal gain, but if you are like me, you want to be available for greater kingdom purposes and to be used by the Master to help build His kingdom…it take resources to do that.

---

[58] Hoffower, Hillary. "We Did the Math to Calculate How Much Money Jeff Bezos Makes in a Year, Month, Week, Day, Hour, Minute, and Second." *Business Insider*, Business Insider, 9 Jan. 2019, www.businessinsider.com/what-amazon-ceo-jeff-bezos-makes-every-day-hour-minute-2018-10.

Reflection

1. Quick Summary

2. Key Insights

3. Personal Application

4. Meaningful Quotes

WEEK 43

Feeling Stuck

Feeling stuck? Everyone goes through those times of feeling like they're in a rut. Here is a simple three-step process to quickly get unstuck.

This quick formula has been a great asset to me for getting out of the ditch that we all find ourselves in at times.

1. *You must clearly define the problem or situation to someone you trust.* Often, when you begin to explain the situation, clarity comes. Because you are so familiar with the situation, you overlook the details in your mind when you are just thinking about it. But when you're forced to explain it to someone who won't judge you but will genuinely probe and seek to understand, it will force you to clarify the situation more fully. It's called the "whiteboard effect." When you have conversations with another person about the issue, solutions present themselves that otherwise would have never revealed on their own.

2. *You have to get centered.* We tend to get caught up in the hustle and bustle of life. We are so busy "human doing" that we forget we are a "human being." We have no time to be still and know that He is God. You must *prioritize* times of *prayer* and, more important, *listening*. For me, it is early in the morning or late at night when everyone is asleep, the phone is not ringing, and email is silent. I can be still, and get with God and not only pray but also sit and be quiet and listen. I am amazed at how many people pray to God like they're making a quick phone call. They will tell God all of their problems and what they want, then seemingly hang up the phone and go about their day. The most important part of prayer is stopping and listening to God's response. The world calls it mindfulness. I call it PUSH—Pray Until Something Happens.

3. *You have to ask yourself WWJD.* We all know the Christianese lingo of "WWJD"—What would Jesus do? But believe it or not, asking this question is a critical part of getting unstuck. Whenever you're stuck in a situation, think about it: What would Jesus do? And not in the cliché way, but really think about it. And visualize what you think He would do. Then take it one step further. If there is someone you know and respect, ask yourself what that person would do. Please understand that the ideas that will come to you are really coming from you—even though you may be visualizing someone else helping you. It's your brain that is offering the solutions. Have you ever given someone else great advice, and you wonder, where did that come from? It's because you were able to detach from the situation and be more objective when you're dealing with someone else's problems rather than your own.

Don't worry; we all get stuck from time to time. The issue is not how many times you get stuck; it is how many times you get *unstuck* and keep it moving. If you have ever gotten stuck and overcome it, share your story of how you got unstuck with someone else who may benefit from your experience. That's one of the marks of a true leader.

Reflection

1. Quick Summary

2. Key Insights

3. Personal Application

4. Meaningful Quotes

WEEK 44

Institutional Imperative

In a 1990 letter to Berkshire Hathaway shareholders, CEO Warren Buffett coined the term "institutional imperative," defining it as "the tendency of executives to mindlessly imitate the behavior of their peers, no matter how foolish it may be to do so."[59] He was following up on a 1989 letter that outlined certain pitfalls within an organization, such as:

(1) A tendency of organizations to behave like objects following Newton's Law of Motion to stay in motion. Similarly, as an organization gains momentum, it will tend to stay the course, even if the course is wrong.

(2) Just as, according to Parkinson's Law, tasks tend to expand or shrink to fit the time assigned to them, so will an organization expand or shrink, not by purpose-filled direction, but by pure, mindless drift.

(3) Any craving or desire of the organization's leader will be quickly adapted and supported, no matter how foolish it may be.

(4) The tendency to mindlessly imitate the behavior of other similar organizations. The Bible says that those who compare themselves among themselves are not wise. We need to be careful to maintain the correct frame of reference around us. Many people underestimate the reference group they associate with. Whether or not you believe it, those with whom you associate make a difference in your life. If you are the smartest kid in the room, you must change rooms.

I once heard of a pastor who was doing Easter-egg drops from a helicopter. I thought, how cool is that! Supposedly, he was attracting thousands, and I was intrigued. For me, it wasn't about the numbers in the crowd; it was about reaping a harvest for the gospel of Christ. My mentor said to me, "Be careful about what you have to do to get people because you are going to have to continue to do it to keep them."

Not long after that, a staff pastor of a very large church told me that his church had stopped doing their large Easter outreach, which they had been doing for years. They received an abundance of calls from people complaining about them canceling this annual event. Upon further research, they discovered that the people who complained never came to the church nor ever contributed to the organization in any way. They realized that although this event created much fanfare, it bore little fruit.

---

[59] Buffett, Warren. Received by Shareholders of Berkshire Hathaway Inc., *Berkshire Hathaway*, 1990, www.berkshirehathaway.com/letters/1990.html.

That was such a clear message for me, demonstrating that we often get caught up in the trap of comparison and feel compelled to imitate rather than innovate.

Avoiding institutional imperative can be very difficult. Buffett's advice is to work with ethical, trustworthy individuals who can run "businesses that possess decent economic characteristics." His lesson is that right is right even if nobody's doing it, and wrong is wrong even if everybody's doing it. Which reminds me of saying credited to an old Texas Rangers cowboy credo: "No man in the wrong can stand up against a fellow that's in the right and keeps on a-comin'."[60]

Knowing what's right is right and what's wrong is wrong becomes a great compass to lead you in your associations. Because, contrary to what the world may say, good does win!

So here is the application zone:

The next time you hold a meeting with your staff or team, don't lead with what you think. Wait and let them talk it through while you drive the discussion, ask questions, and probe. If you lead with your ideas, most people who support you will just go along with you. It creates "confirmation bias." In other words, your people will just confirm and support your ideas without ever positing any new and innovative ideas.

In what areas of business can you step out and find another ethical and trustworthy reference group (even if it's outside of your particular industry or ministry)?

Whom do you know who may be successful in some other area, someone who may be a good person to connect with?

When an organization grows more than 20 percent, systems need to be changed and reevaluated.

- What systems and programs are on drift?
- What are you doing only because you saw someone else do it?
- Are there things you do just because you've been doing them and continue doing them because that's just the way things were done in the past?

---

[60] Weiser-Alexander, Kathy. "William Jesse McDonald- U.S. Deputy Marshal & Texas Ranger." *Legends of America*, 2020, www.legendsofamerica.com/william-mcdonald/.

Week 44: Institutional Imperative

Reflection

1. Quick Summary

2. Key Insights

3. Personal Application

4. Meaningful Quotes

WEEK 45

Kidpreneur

As a young man, *Shark Tank* investor Daymond John sold customized pencils to the prettiest girls at school. The venture was rather successful until the principal shut it down because John was stealing the pencils from boys he didn't like.

At the age of twelve, John's fellow *Shark Tank* investor Mark Cuban desired a pair of expensive sneakers. He went door to door, selling trash bags in order to raise the capital.

As a young boy, Warren Buffett, the "Oracle of Omaha," bought packs of gum from his grandfather's store then went door to door selling them to his neighbors. When one woman wanted to buy one stick, he replied, "We don't break up the packs."

An 11-year-old Richard Branson bred parakeets and sold them as pets.[61]

The list goes on. Many of the world's most successful people started some level of enterprise at a young age. I had a few entrepreneurial experiences in my childhood, including shoveling snow, raking leaves, mowing lawns, detailing cars, and various other enterprises. When I was 11 and in middle school, I ran a candy business. Some of my greatest business lessons came from that endeavor.

We had just moved, and I had begun school in a new neighborhood in a whole new town. Right next to my school in my previous neighborhood, a corner store called Mary's sold candy, chips, and all kinds of stuff. But my new neighborhood had no such store within walking distance of the school. The first thing I learned was to identify deficiencies in the market.

When you do the research and identify an unmet or untapped need, you will always find opportunities. With just that quick idea, a candy business was born. I discussed this opportunity to start my side hustle with my parents. They told me I would have to save the money I made in a bank account, and I had to assure them that my grades would not slip.

I learned two great principles right there. One, when you start a side hustle that is not capable of replacing your primary source of income, you must *guard against allowing it to cause your primary source of income to suffer*.

---

[61] Baer, Drake. "9 Legendary Entrepreneurs Who Started When They Were Kids." *Business Insider*, Business Insider, 27 Nov. 2014, www.businessinsider.com/entrepreneurs-who-started-their-first-business-as-kids-2014-11.

Two, if you want to be successful in the long term, you must develop a habit of *saving for your future*. Remember, you haven't paid yourself until you have saved money in the bank.

With my parents on board and a plan in my little head, I initially bought a bunch of candy at a local store and began selling it at school. It sold out quickly. Then, thirdly, I realized that *if I purchased in bulk from the warehouse store, I could get my product much cheaper*.

Tip number four: Always find ways to decrease costs. This is a very simple formula for success when it comes to business—*Revenue must exceed expenses*. You must always be mindful of two functions: *increasing sales* and *decreasing expenses*.

Speaking of controlling costs, as a little kid who loved candy, I shorted my profits by eating some of that candy myself, which is a great segue to tip number five: *Never get high on your own supply*.

Now I was making a couple of hundred dollars a week selling candy. As the word spread, so did the sales. While my candy cost kids more than what they would pay at the store, I provided a convenience that justified my premium charge.

That leads me to tip number six: Being the cheapest is not always the way to win customers. As a matter of fact, if you provide convenience or high-quality service, people are inclined to pay a premium.

As news spread, a few others started to compete with my business. Which brings me to lesson number seven: Never fear competition, as any time you are on to a great idea, the competition will arise. People see what you do and think it looks easy. But they don't realize what you have already learned from mistakes that they have yet to learn. Remember, no one can do what you do.

Here's the part I am not proud of. A kid started moving in on my territory, so I paid some upperclassmen to troll him and take his candy and shut him down. I paid them with not only the spoils of their conquest but also with free candy from my stores for the next few weeks. Very *Godfather*-ish and Mafia-esque. I'm sorry about that incident. I'm glad I am saved now. Thank God, I am forgiven in Christ! Oh, the sins of our youth—

As the word spread, the principal called me to his office and told me that any candy I had sold in school would have to be for the benefit of fundraising. Much like Daymond John with his pencil business, I was shut down by the principal. In other words, the "capos" wanted their cut of my profits. It was a good run, but I had to cease and desist because this 11-year-old boy was not going to capitulate to La Cosa Nostra. Lesson number eight: When you start doing well, everybody wants a cut of the action.

The final and greatest lesson was learning to understand entrepreneurship and the thrill of making my way and providing something people need. I am grateful to my parents and my older brother, who taught me to engage in the entrepreneurial rollercoaster.

I would love to hear from you about ventures you may have undertaken as a kid and lessons you learned from it. Join our Facebook Group, #LEVELUP, to share your story. I look forward to reading your responses.

Reflection

1. Quick Summary

2. Key Insights

3. Personal Application

4. Meaningful Quotes

WEEK 46

Leading in a Time of Crisis

In light of recent world events, we have seen times of great distress and pandemonium. I wanted to remind you that this is a time in which leadership is greatly needed. In times of crisis, we, as leaders, are called to help bring peace and settle the hearts and minds of those we serve—our customers, our donors, supporters, clients, employees, and whomever else you may lead.

Below are three of the five C's you need to focus on:

The First C Is *Certainty*.

As a leader, you have the voice and the influence to bring certainty. The reason for panic is rooted in those who control the narratives. We are a resilient people, and truthfully, we will get through every crisis, even COVID-19, as we have in the past. By way of comparison, many years ago, smallpox killed over half a billion people. That was a time of great unrest and crisis. Regardless of the situation, we have to understand and make it our "mantra" that "this, too, shall pass."

Bring certainty to your teams and to those around you by *not speaking to the condition*, but *speaking life to the direction that moves beyond the crisis* and call "those things that are not as though they are."

The Second C Is *Creativity*.

To the trained eye, times of great *unrest* are times of great *opportunity*. Over half of the top 30 Dow companies started in times of great turmoil. Now is a time to recognize opportunity and potential. You need to spend this time being creative in coming up with opportunities for you to grow and succeed. *I am not talking about exploitation but innovation.* We don't take advantage of people, but I assure you, there is an opportunity for innovation in these times. You just have to commit to being resourceful and creative.

God has not given us the spirit of fear but of love, power, and a sound mind. A sound mind solves problems and creates solutions. You may have to pivot in your business. There are creative opportunities abounding. Figure them out and make the adjustments. Maybe consider new delivery systems for your products and services. In this time, technology is so developed that the possibilities are endless—just commit yourself to finding them. You will be shocked at the ideas and solutions that come your way when you are truly committed.

The Third C Is *Clarity*.

In times of controversy, confusion reigns. In James 3:16, the Bible says, "For where envying and strife is, there is confusion and every evil work."

Seek to clarify and differentiate your organization. In *The Art of War*, Sun Tzu says that if you are smaller, then you need to be faster. If you're a small organization, exploit your strengths and outmaneuver your competition. Seek to clarify your branding, clarify your communications, clarify your message. Set yourself apart and bring clarity as to why you are the premier organization to continue doing business with. This is a time to get clear with your staff and your clients. Don't be cute; be clear.

Reflection

1. Quick Summary

2. Key Insights

3. Personal Application

4. Meaningful Quotes

WEEK 47

Leading in a Time of Crisis - Part 2

In the last chapter, we discussed the first three of the five C's you need to focus on. Now, we will talk about the remaining two.

The Fourth C Is *Conciseness.*

Simplify. Simplify. Simplify.

Simplify everything. Make it easy for your employees and your clients. Research the problem. Get the info for them and simplify it and disseminate it to them. Help them to process all that is going on, then rally them in the right direction. But remember to *KISS*—Keep It Simple, Stupid. Break it down to its irreducible minimums for them and influence them toward the correct narrative.

The Last and Most Important C Is *Christ.*

I saved the best for last. Sometimes people think that God is not interested in the way we make a living. That is simply untrue. If you look back at the apostles and those God used throughout the Bible, you will see many business people and leaders who were used for the glory of God.

Please understand that in times of great crisis, we need to seek the leadership of the Holy Ghost. You must know that if God be for you, then who can stand against you? He has and will continue to bless the work of your hands. And when this season has passed, and all is said and done, you will have been in the furnace, but not have gotten burned, and you won't even smell like smoke. God is still on the throne.

Since I am a bit of an overachiever, here is a sixth C: *Cultivate.*

Recently, we as a nation have found ourselves with more time on our hands than expected. This season has provided the hours to spend developing and cultivating skills or finally reading that book or working on that project we never seem to be able to get around to. The best time to do these things is now. You don't want to try to learn how to swim while you're drowning. You must invest in your growth and development. Don't get caught off guard being too busy.

You may say, "I don't have time for that," or "I'm too busy right now." Abraham Lincoln is quoted saying, "Give me six hours to chop down a tree, and I will spend the first four sharpening the ax." You are the ax for your organization, so you must sharpen the saw. Invest in your growth and development in the areas that matter the most—not just-in-case learning, but just-in-time learning, not things that you may never use or need but things that you can implement immediately, and that will help you cut down that tree a lot easier.

If you haven't considered our LeaderSHIFT Success Masterclass, I would strongly suggest it. That way, in the crisis, you don't have to spend a moment worrying. Instead, you'll be able to focus on the important so you can do the impossible.

Reflection

1. Quick Summary

2. Key Insights

3. Personal Application

4. Meaningful Quotes

WEEK 48

Retail Apocalypse

You will not believe the list of businesses that closed their doors in 2019.

In 2018, 6,000 stores in the US went out of business. The analysts and pundits have coined a new phrase: The Retail Apocalypse.[62] We seem to be mirroring what Charles Dickens wrote in *A Tale of Two Cities*:[63]

It was the best of times, it was the worst of times, it was the age of wisdom, it was the age of foolishness, it was the epoch of belief, it was the epoch of incredulity, it was the season of light, it was the season of darkness, it was the spring of hope, it was the winter of despair.

If you thought 2018 was a low point for brick-and-mortar retailers, think again. Sadly, 2019 proved to be exponentially more brutal, and Coresight Research predicted the number of store closures would double from the numbers of 2018 and would reach a staggering 12,000 by the year's end—from Payless Shoes to Party City, GNC to Bed Bath & Beyond. Shopping malls these days look like something straight out of a zombie apocalypse movie.

Check out this list of the most notable victims of the retail apocalypse in 2019: (It will shock you!

Company	Stores Closed (or Closing)
Payless ShoeSource	2,500
GNC	900
Gymboree and Crazy 8	805
Dressbarn	650
Fred's	568
Charlotte Russe	500
Family Dollar	390
Shopko	370

---

[62] Wikipedia contributors. "Retail apocalypse." *Wikipedia, The Free Encyclopedia*. Wikipedia, The Free Encyclopedia, 23 Jul. 2020. Web. 23 Jul. 2020.

[63] Dickens, Charles, and De Mille A. B. *A Tale of Two Cities*. Allyn and Bacon, 1966.

Company (continued)	Stores Closed (or Closing)
Things Remembered	274
Charming Charlie	260
Chico's	250
Gap	230
Avenue	222
Walgreens	200
GameStop	200
Destination Maternity	183
Forever 21	178
LifeWay Christian	170
Kitchen Collection	160
Kay, Zales, and Jareds (Signet Jewelers)	150
Sears and Kmart	121
Performance Bicycle	104
Bed Bath & Beyond (Buy Buy Baby and Cost Plus World Market)	60
Pier 1 Imports	57
Party City	55
Victoria's Secret	53
Office Depot	50

When a study was conducted to determine the cause of these tragic retail failures, in most cases, the problem was a lack of customers.

Today's retail markets are very competitive, and people are moving online to shop. There seems to be a trend of organizations not caring about customer service; for that reason, many consumers have made the decision to buy online. With some of the largest organizations working diligently to decrease shipping times—some even offering same-day delivery—it has become easier to shop online and bypass shoddy customer service for ease, simplicity, and, in some instances, lower prices.

If you want to survive and thrive in your business, you will have to revisit and map out your customer experience. Many organizations don't need a business plan; they need a customer plan.

According to a recent poll, people are still willing to pay a premium for quality. In fact, the price premium for quality among consumers worldwide is up to 16% for products and services. The report was based on 15,000 global respondents. The survey found that 42% of consumers said they would pay up to 16% more for a friendly, welcoming experience, and 52% would pay more for a speedy and efficient customer experience.

Of course, price and quality are still the top considerations when consumers make a purchase decision. However, 73% said that a good experience is key in influencing their brand loyalties.[64]

There is a rush in the market to be the cheapest. I assure you, this trend is a fad and will soon fail. You must find ways to differentiate yourself to win in this market. You have to focus on new ways to "deliver the goods," so to speak. People want quality. And in a world of chatbots and email, customer service is creating a gap and void in the marketplace that can be filled by someone with imagination, creativity, and a penchant for quality service.

So, resist the urge to compete on a price level. You know as well as I do that no good thing is cheap and no cheap thing is good. Always bear in mind that *value* and *price* are *not synonymous*. Seek ways to increase the value of what you offer before ever talking about its price. Often, if you are creative, you'll find many inexpensive ways to increase value while mainstreaming your price.

One of the reasons we started the LeaderSHIFT Success Masterclass was to help ministry and business leaders stay fully funded and grow in a world that seems to be eating up the competition.

Proverbs 22:29 says, "Do you see a man skillful in his work? He will stand before kings; he will not stand before obscure men."

There is a reason why some of the top premier brands in the world have lasted for decades through recessions, through good times and bad—because they have a strategy that is timeless.

The LeaderSHIFT Success Masterclass takes a behind-the-scenes look at the secret playbook of some of the most successful brands in the business. There is a reason they are successful and have stood the test of time. If you are interested in being part of an upcoming masterclass, join our Facebook Group, #LEVELUP, to get the details of this event. One idea we shared from this event made us 18K and still counting, and it cost us about $400.

Take the time to learn the skills and tactics to ensure the longevity of your organization. We are so confident that we even offer a full money-back guarantee, so you have nothing to lose. Take the time to invest in your business. You will be glad you did.

---

[64] Clark, David, and Ron Kinghorn. "Experience Is Everything: Here's How to Get It Right." *PwC*, 2018, www.pwc.com/future-of-cx.

Reflection

1. Quick Summary

2. Key Insights

3. Personal Application

4. Meaningful Quotes

WEEK 49

May I Take Your Order, Please?

If your presence is required for the business to run well, you have a job and not a business.

My wife went to Wendy's drive-thru some time back. She was met with a handwritten note stating they were out of Dr. Pepper, tomato, barbecue dip, honey mustard, ranch, and chicken nuggets. (Dear God, what is left at that point?) When she got to the window she inquired as to the problem. They said the manager was on vacation.

The litmus test to being a business owner is whether or not you are required to be present for things to function properly. Let me say it this way. If your presence is necessary for the business to run well, then you have a job and not a business. You are an employee and not an owner. While this is jarring to some, it is a definite truth. More importantly, it is the key to scale. Could you imagine Apple—who, by the way, makes $127 million per day—closing its doors with the passing of Steve Jobs, or shutting down for the week because the CEO is home sick with the flu?

As a Ministry or business leader, you should be developing someone to handle every area of your organization. When you consider this Wendy's debacle, you can see there were several problems. Not only was the organization crippled, but it shows poor leadership and development on the part of the manager. It also shows that the standards are not even held. At a minimum, who posts a handwritten note? It could have at least been typed up on a computer. I am not trying to be critical but trying to illustrate that people need to have your heart and your hands. Everything they do represents the organization and leaves an impression on your customer.

Have you ever sat back and thought about what systems and processes would drift if you were not present? I am a person of faith, so I don't want my words to trip me up; however, what if something happened to you? Do you have a system of checks and balances? Is there repetition in place to ensure the future success of the organization you lead, not just for your enterprise but for your family and those you lead? As a leader, you cannot afford to derive your sense of worth from knowing everything. If you are not careful, you will begin to hoard knowledge that is needed in other levels of the company for the sake of avoiding internally perceived feelings of obsolescence.

You must have the confidence to know that you were fearfully and wonderfully made. No one can do the assignment God has given you, but people need to be trained on how to do the tasks so you can take a vacation. Treat yourself to some well-deserved rest. As Vince Lombardi said, "We win our games in practice." The time to train people is when you are in "practice" so that when you go live, people are ready to step in and win!

Here is a final word of caution:

You have to be careful of familiarity. Since you do what you do all the time, it has become second nature. You may not be able to recognize what needs to be taught until you are on vacation or otherwise out of the loop, so to speak. It is much like a windshield. You don't know it's not there until it is missing. While driving along in our cars, we take it for granted that a windshield blocks the wind and keeps the bugs out of your teeth until there is no more windshield. There is a popular story that a COO asked the CEO this question: "What if we train our people so well that they leave us?" to which the CEO replied, "What happens if we don't, and they stay?"

Richard Branson, I believe, offers the best answer to this dilemma. He said, "Train people so well that they can leave, and treat them well enough that they don't want to."

Spend time thinking it through. Ask your employees what they may feel is important for them to know how to do. Do not allow insecurities to drive these discussions, and you will be well on your way to scale.

Reflection

1. Quick Summary

2. Key Insights

3. Personal Application

4. Meaningful Quotes

WEEK 50

12 Key Attributes of Elite Team Players

In the chapters to follow, I have assembled the key traits and characteristics of our team at Leadership Uncensored. These are the core traits and characteristics of who we are and whom we strive to be. They drive us each and every day. The word character comes from two root words—*char* "to burn," and *actor,* "to act." What is burned into you will determine how you act. Adversity does not build character; it merely reveals it. These characteristics are how we gauge our culture and success. They are the measuring stick by which we reward, promote, and, if need be, liberate members back into the workplace. Since you have made it this far, I am certain that you are made of A-Grade material, or you wouldn't be here in the first place. Each one of our 12 elite team characteristics is briefly detailed in the following chapters.

Our first attribute of our elite world-class team is to be *Obsessively Fastidious*. We have an almost obsessive-compulsive commitment to excellence—the details matter.

Song of Solomon 2:15 NASB reads," Catch the foxes for us, the little foxes that are ruining the vineyards, while our vineyards are in blossom."

It is often the small foxes that spoil the vine. We are thorough in our execution, striving at all times for a high bar of accuracy and excellence. Having extreme ownership, we quickly correct our own mistakes and do not pass around monkeys. We have a serious commitment to ownership and pay strict attention to the details.

Everything we do is executed in this order:
1. Excellent first
2. Fast second
3. Then finally, Price.

Excellence and speed are always the top priorities, but we do not sacrifice excellence for speed or price.

Our second attribute of our elite team is *Ridiculous Creativity and Resourcefulness*. Exodus 35:35 reads, "He has filled them with the skill to do all kinds of work as engravers, designers, embroiderers in blue, purple and scarlet yarn and fine linen, and weavers—all of them skilled workers and designers." God has graced us with abilities, a spirit of wisdom, and a mind to work. Therefore, solving problems is what we do. Maintaining the correct attitude and focus, not only to get out of the box but also to create on a level that there is no box.

People tend to forget that your pay is determined by the size of the problems you know how to solve. The very nature of leadership is a person solving a problem in a situation where all of the resources are not present to accomplish a task or goal. It takes a person of certainty and commitment to become resourceful and knows that there is always a solution. We have the Holy Ghost residing on the inside of us, and that makes us the smartest kids in the room. With God's help, all things are possible. We are committed to The Rule of Three; if you don't have three options, then you don't really have a choice. When it comes to effective problem solving, we are committed to finding three options. One option is no choice; Two options are a dilemma. Three options allow us to make a decision. Maintaining the standard of requiring three options forces a higher and deeper level of creative thinking. It is easy to come up with one choice. It is harder to find three viable options, and often in this pursuit, you will find that one (or a combination) of your options will be the right choice.

Our third attribute of our elite team is to be a *Passionate Follower, Not A Fan*. Jeff Holden, who has held high-level positions with Amazon, Groupon, and Uber, is quoted saying, "Wars are won by patriots, not mercenaries." You can start a war with mercenaries, but you will not win a war with mercenaries

The difference between a patriot and a mercenary is that a mercenary is paid to care. Patriots are violently passionate about the work they do and the impact they get to make. We are passionate about the mission. We behave like owners of the brand, vision, and mission. We are not renters who always have one foot out the door. Mercenaries are detrimental for truly sustainable growth.

I have been careful to step you through this process because many mercenaries are good at saying the right things to make them seem value-aligned, which is why we run a series of culture fit tests to see if actions back up their words.

We are enthusiastic about the opportunity to serve God and are grateful for the privilege it is to make a kingdom impact. We know that there is an eternal reward for the eternal work that we do. It is a privilege and an honor to do meaningful work. We are enthusiastic about the privilege the Lord Jesus has bestowed upon us to serve him. The word enthusiasm comes from two Greek words, *en* and *theos* meaning "in God". This next attribute is of a dying breed in today's world. That attribute is *Unbreakable Resilience*. There is IQ (Intelligence Quotient), ie. Smarts!, EQ (Emotional Quotient), or the aptitude be relational, and AQ (Adversity Quotient), the ability to endure. We are fearless and determined with the grit and resolve to overcome every obstacle and turn it into an opportunity. Many would buckle under the pressure we can endure as we continue to push back the forces of darkness. We are clear that we are a force for good and God. We are load bearers in every sense of the term. We can carry loads by God's grace that others cannot because we are anointed and appointed for such a time as this.

Our fifth attribute is the key to our core value of impact. It is to be *Smart on a Gifted Level*. Not only are we intelligent, but we possess the wisdom to apply the information in a way that produces above-average results. We understand how to work smart. We seek CANEI (Constant and never-ending improvement). Gen. George

S. Patton is quoted saying, "A pint of sweat will save a gallon of blood."[65] We understand that the key to scale and our effectiveness is rooted in our ability to create, assess, modify, improve, and/or abandon outdated systems while creating higher efficiency levels for the organizations. We accomplish our goals with the least amount of effort by finding the leverage (or sweet spot, so to speak) created when you have great systems designed to produce maximum output. The idea is to work smarter, not harder by becoming masters at planning, and then executing with speed and precision. Statistics say that hiring a key elite player is the equivalent of hiring three average players.

Our sixth key attribute of an elite team member is more an art than science, and that is to be *Confidently Assertive.* Arrogance and confidence are often confused. We are confident and will assert ourselves to constructively input where needed boldly and authentically to bring about the organization's greater good. We understand the difference between being critical and constructive. We will not be silent and allow our organizations, team, or leaders to fail. We know when to speak up or step in for the greater common good of the organizations that God has entrusted to us.

---

[65] "Quotes - Information and Licensing for General Patton." *General Patton*, www.generalpatton.com/quotes/.

Reflection

1. Quick Summary

2. Key Insights

Week 50: 12 Key Attributes of Elite Team Players

3. Personal Application

4. Meaningful Quotes

WEEK 51

12 Key Attributes of Elite Team Players - Part 2

The seventh attribute is one that I believe you either have or you don't. That is *Earnest Empathy*: we have a deep love for what we do (the work), whom we get to do it with (the Team), and for whom we get to do it for (members/our clients). We are diligent in expending the effort to earnestly care for and tangibly display empathy to empower not only our brothers in sisters in Christ but also the world in which we live. We seek to make a greater impact on our sphere of influence at all times, allowing us to be genuine and authentic as we care about and for the world around us. Not just for gain but truly for the betterment of those around us regardless of our perceived return. It is far better to give than to receive.

This is probably the attribute that I pray about the most and seek God's will and direction on the most often. That is to be *Faith-Filled and Faithful*. There is a difference between being faithful and faith-filled. Being faithful (2 Sam 2:30) is doing things the way that it is in our leaders' hearts and minds. Being full of faith means we are in a constant state of expectation and belief as we release our faith to accomplish the God-sized dream that our organizations are meant to fulfill. We are proficient in the Spirit, not only our godly discernment but also skillful enough to operate under the leadership and direction of the Holy Ghost while bringing a supply of faith to what we do to accomplish God-sized results. The Spirit of God is our great advantage.

I believe attribute number nine is the "secret sauce" to success. We are *Reliably Consistent*. The difference between an amateur and a professional is consistency. Regardless of the situation, we aim to constantly adhere to the same set of guiding principles, behavior, standards, attitude, and quality. We are predictably predictable, steady, reliable, and dependable. Can you imagine what it would be like if Tiger Woods was inconsistent in every championship tournament he played, or if Micheal Jordan could not be dependable? In 1997 — Game 5 of the NBA Finals between the Chicago Bulls and Utah Jazz, became known as the "Flu Game".[66] On the bench, A very sick Micheal Jordan leaned far back in his seat with ice packs on his head while chugging fluids. As ill as Jordan was, however, it didn't keep him from being reliable. In Chicago's 90-88 win, the ailing Jordan recorded an unbelievable 38

---

[66] Dodson, Aaron. "On This Day in NBA Finals History: Michael Jordan's 'Flu Game'." *The Undefeated*, The Undefeated, 11 June 2017, theundefeated.com/features/nba-finals-history-michael-jordan-flu-game/.

points, 7 rebounds, 5 assists, 3 steals and 1 block, including a 3-pointer with less than a minute left. That gave the Bulls the lead that they did not relinquish.

To be *Reliably Consistent* means we play at the same level for every game. We do not allow other people's standards to sway ours. We go hard in the paint, knowing that, as Colossians 3:23 says, "Whatever you do, work at it with all your heart, as working for the Lord, not for human masters"

Number ten in our list of key attributes for our elite team is an *Outrageous Sense of URGENCY.* We must be efficient in our processes and thinking to move at the speed of light. In today's world of super High-Speed information, people expect speed. We are capable of demonstrating that people matter and that our work is important enough to us that we MOVE with Genesis-level speed to accomplish God-sized goals. After all, God created the whole world in only six days. Parkinson's Law tells us that tasks expand to the time you allow for it. That means if you think it's going to take forever, it will! If you give yourself shorter deadlines and truly believe that you can accomplish it, you will be amazed at what can be done in less time. It is important to realize that we must think on a Genesis speed level if we are going to have a competitive edge. We as believers are working ultimately for the cause of Christ; we have an anointing to help.

We are in the final stretch with our last two attributes of a high-performance elite team. Number eleven is to be *High Growth*. Great leaders are not born; they are made. We are extremely committed to learning and growing. Benjamin Franklin said, "If a man empties his purse into his head, no man can take it away from him. An investment in knowledge always pays the best interest." Not only are we humble enough to be teachable, but we are able to lead ourselves to implement and grow ourselves, never becoming complacent with mediocrity and the status quo and ever-challenging ourselves to learn and grow by actively seeking resources to expand or knowledge and increase our abilities. Jim Rohn has said that you don't achieve big goals; you grow into them. There is a quote that says if you think education is expensive, try the cost of ignorance.

Last but not certainly not least in our list of elite team member attributes is to focus on being *High Performance or (5E)*. This means we have a relentless commitment to *Excellence, Effectiveness, Efficiency, Execution,* & being *Extraordinary*. "5E" is a framework that exemplifies five key qualities of our performance. We are committed to

1. **Excellence:** the greatest enemy of best if good enough. It is never good enough. Excellence is not perfection. Excellence is doing the best we can with what we have.
2. **Effectiveness**: Movement and being effective are not the same. We have the ability to discern that being busy is not the same as being effective. We must be relentless at determining what is unjustified motion and what is progress. When one sits in a rocking chair, they are moving, but they are not going anywhere. We possess a remarkable ability to assess and refine effort to produce the result.

3. **Efficiency:** Winning by brute force is never the answer; it causes massive exhaustion on a wide organizational scale. We must learn to leverage our time in an effective way to understand what is important and focus most of our efforts efficiently on the tasks that produce the greatest results. This is more art than science and requires IQ and EQ to ensure that our effort produces maximum results effectively

4. **Execution:** Larry Bossidy, the author of the book *Execution: The Discipline of Gettings Things Done*, said, "To execute well, there must be accountability, clear goals, accurate methods to measure performance, and the right rewards for people who perform." It doesn't matter if we have a great strategy that poorly executes. The result is catastrophic. However, if we have a good plan and execute it well, we will create momentum and see extraordinary results

5. **Extraordinary:** Extraordinary is defined as going beyond what is usual, regular, or customary. We strive to shatter expectations by not being just good, but great. There is a temptation of laziness and apathy that propagates the idea of just getting by. We seek moments and occasions to be extraordinary, going above and beyond the norm. Finding ways to go above and beyond the call of duty.

Reflection

1. Quick Summary

2. Key Insights

3. Personal Application

4. Meaningful Quotes

WEEK 52

Why We Do What We Do

At this point in the book, I want to have a Leadership Uncensored heart-to-heart, a family meeting of sorts. You may be wondering, What's the point?

It all started about ten years ago. (I feel like Sophia from *The Golden Girls*. "It all started in 1962, Sicily…" Ha-ha.)

Seriously, now, about ten years ago, a theme started to grace the headlines of many secular magazines and newspapers—yeah, I know I said "newspapers."

There was a leadership crisis on the horizon back then. According to one recent study, over 70% of companies do not feel that their leaders can lead their organization into the future. Only 10% of leadership positions have a ready, willing, and able successor.[67] Although it should not be this way, but as unfortunate as this is, it is a truth of today's world: Whenever the world sneezes, the church catches a cold.

There is a leadership crisis in both the world and in the church.

- Over half of senior ministry leaders report that their seminary did not prepare them for the ministry.
- Just under 40% of senior ministry leaders battle fatigue, depression, or fear of inadequacy.
- 80% of leaders and 84% of their spouses have felt unqualified and discouraged.
- 1 out of every 10 pastors will actually retire as a pastor.
- Over 50% of ministries say they struggle with finding leaders.[68]

There is a leadership crisis, and we at Leadership Uncensored are looking to equip and empower the next generation of leaders.

You may notice that we don't promote any particular church or denomination; we remain neutral. We provide the tools, clarity, and confidence to help leaders level up their leadership. We desire to provide pragmatic and valuable Christ-centered tools to help gain leverage and increase effectiveness and efficiency in any organization, business, or ministry.

The systems and strategies, if you will, are from the playbook of some of the GOATs (the Greatest Of All Time)—strategies of the best and brightest top-performing ministries and businesses to give you clarity and focus. Often, as people

---

[67] Velasquez, Robert. "13 Shocking Leadership Development Statistics (Infographic)." *Infopro Learning*, 15 Aug. 2019, www.infoprolearning.com/infographic/13-shocking-leadership-development-statistics-infopro-learning/.

[68] *Statistics for Pastors*, www.pastoralcareinc.com/statistics/.

focus on the mundane, they forget about the mighty, that is, the true purpose behind what they do and why.

We truly desire to help you gain the confidence to not sin against your God-given talent and ability. We know that an equipped warrior is a confident warrior. Together, we can take back territory for Christ.

Our desire is to provide so much value that it incites growth and cultivates ideas for breakthrough thinking and quantum-leap transformation. This may sound somewhat bizarre, but I have easily spent (or known companies that spend) 100K on conferences, books, seminars, and learning opportunities to gain insight over 25 years of business experience. I have also learned more in my 15 years of ministerial experience. Everything I paid to learn has its roots in the Bible. I wish I had known 30 years ago that all of the top principles of business are represented in the Word of God.

Here at Leadership Uncensored, we understand that a war has been waged against leadership. As former Saints defensive coordinator Gregg Williams said, "Kill the head and the body will die." That saying was plastered on the wall in the Chiefs' defensive-line meeting room, and it was the first thing every player saw whenever they walked in.

We simply cannot lose our leadership in our Christian organizations.

We have endeavored to uncover and connect these truths so that you can apply them easily to your business and ministry in order to start taking back territory for the cause of Christ.

We have a God-sized dream of influencing 90 million potential leaders and influencers around the world, and we need your help to get there. We know that, over their lifespan, the average leader will affect, on average, over 300 people, and each of those people will affect another 300.

While 90 million may be a God-sized goal, it is also God-possible. Will you help us accomplish this goal and turn the tide of lethargic leadership in the Body of Christ? First and foremost, please pray for us. Second, if our Leadercasts or other resources and programs have been a blessing to you, pay it forward and share them with other leaders. We need one another. Let the spirit of help and cooperation drive you to be a blessing to someone else. You never know what they may need. And lastly, communicate with us and let us know if this is blessing you and how we can improve. Feedback is the breakfast of champions!

Week 52: Why We Do What We Do

BOOK DR. GENE HERNDON
BIOGRAPHY

Dr. Gene Herndon, or as he is called by many, Dr. G. is a Senior Pastor, Itinerant Minister and Conference Speaker, Thought Leader, Serial Entrepreneur, Best-Selling Author, Publisher, Educator, and most importantly a devoted husband and father. As if that isn't enough, he is always looking to expand his holdings and interests in business branding, marketing, consulting, entertainment, and beyond.

His entrepreneurial bug started early in life (in middle school to be exact). He quickly learned that sales and entrepreneurship set the path to economic freedom.

Having close to 30 years of experience, his executive background spans both domestic and international c-level business experiences, ranging from designing and launching startup ventures to corporate turnarounds. As an entrepreneur and corporate executive, he has worked for, acquired, built, and sold several businesses ranging from real estate and finance, to information technology.

His voracious appetite for learning sparked a development journey early in his career that not only earned him a Doctorate in Divinity (D. Div.) but also drove him to easily invest over six figures in conferences, classes, and books on the the subjects of business and leadership. Having curated many principles and keys that he learned along the way allowed him to become known for his ability to successfully integrate the right strategies and tactics into well-executed operating plans, building strong teams and achieving superior results. As a prolific author, he has written twelve books on subjects of leadership and theology designed to promote growth for the body of Christ.

He holds a firm belief that a standard of excellence is the key to preeminence. As an industry leader, best-selling author, and ground breaking entrepreneurial expert, he has honed and evolved into a highly sought-after business, motivational and ministry conference speaker.

- SEEKING THE LOST
- TRAINING THE FOUND
- SENDING THE READY
- EQUIPPING THE SENT

Areas Of Expertise

- Entrepreneurship
- Ministry
- Leadership
- Theology
- Productivity
- Business
- Publishing

Connect With Dr. Gene

GENE@GENEHERNDON.com

Free Weekly Mentoring
m4.geneherndon.com

Main Website
www.GeneHerndon.com

Suggested Topics for Media Interviews
Why volunteers have to be led, not managed.
The top mind shifts of the wealthy.
The key to recruiting key players.
The greatest parasite of productivity.
Ten ways to guarantee startup success.

FREE Weekly Mentoring

Visit m4.GeneHerndon.com

Increase your business
Advance your career
Grow your ministry

An intentionally Christ-centered weekly leadercast delivered right to your inbox for corporate visionaries, business and ministry leaders where we take a few minutes every Monday morning to discuss an insightful and practical biblical leadership principle. We quickly distill it and make it easy to apply to give you the tools, clarity, and confidence to lead your business or ministry at the next level.

Every Monday morning through this leadercast, I would like to sit down with you and share one big idea and then give you the whole week to process it, allow God to expand on it, and then if you feel it will help to then implement it.

I am confident that regardless of what level of leadership you are currently in, whether you are in business and or ministry, there will always be one big idea that will help and bless you.

It is our desire to help you with the tools, clarity, and confidence to lead at the next level.

See you Monday morning! Until then, Level Up!

DISCOVER MORE

- Weekly Christ-centered Leadership Mentoring
- Business and Ministry
- Explore Free Resources and Tools
- Locate Live Events
- Podcasts

Other Resources
Available @ geneherndon.com

www.ingramcontent.com/pod-product-compliance
Lightning Source LLC
Chambersburg PA
CBHW080334170426
43194CB00014B/2557